First World War
and Army of Occupation
War Diary
France, Belgium and Germany

62 DIVISION
186 Infantry Brigade
Duke of Wellington's (West Riding Regiment)
2/4th Battalion
9 January 1917 - 28 February 1919

WO95/3086/1

The Naval & Military Press Ltd
www.nmarchive.com
Published in association with The National Archives

Published by

The Naval & Military Press Ltd

Unit 10 Ridgewood Industrial Park,

Uckfield, East Sussex,

TN22 5QE England

Tel: +44 (0) 1825 749494

www.naval-military-press.com

www.nmarchive.com

This diary has been reprinted in facsimile from the original. Any imperfections are inevitably reproduced and the quality may fall short of modern type and cartographic standards.

© Crown Copyright
Images reproduced by permission of The National Archives, London, England, 2015.

Contents

Document type	Place/Title	Date From	Date To
Heading	WO95/3086-1		
Heading	62nd Division 186th Infy Bde 2-4th Duke Of Wellington Regt Jan 1917-1918 Feb		
Heading	War Diary of 2/4th Bn Duke of Wellingtons Regt From 9th January 1917 To 31st January 1917 Volume 1		
War Diary	Southampton	09/01/1917	10/01/1917
War Diary	Havre	11/01/1917	13/01/1917
War Diary	Villers L'Hopital	15/01/1917	23/01/1917
War Diary	Bus	25/01/1917	31/01/1917
Heading	War Diary of 2/4th Bn. Duke of Wellington's Regt. From 1st February 1917 To 28th February 1917 Volume II		
War Diary	Bus	02/02/1917	13/02/1917
War Diary	Trenches	15/02/1917	17/02/1917
War Diary	Mailly Mailly	21/02/1917	25/02/1917
War Diary	Mailly Wood E	26/02/1917	26/02/1917
Heading	War Diary of 2/4th Bn Duke of Wellingtons Regt From 1st March 1917 To 31st March 1917 Volume 3		
War Diary	Y Ravine Beaumont Hamel	01/03/1917	04/03/1917
War Diary	Forceville	06/03/1917	14/03/1917
War Diary	Beaumont Hamel	15/03/1917	15/03/1917
War Diary	In The Field	16/03/1917	28/03/1917
Heading	War Diary of 2/4 Bn Duke of Wellingtons Regt From 1st April 1917 To 30th April 1917 Volume 4		
War Diary	Achiet-Le Petit	06/04/1917	06/04/1917
War Diary	Ervillers	08/04/1917	11/04/1917
War Diary	Mory	12/04/1917	12/04/1917
War Diary	Ecoust	13/04/1917	18/04/1917
War Diary	Mory	19/04/1917	19/04/1917
War Diary	B 26 Central	20/04/1917	20/04/1917
Operation(al) Order(s)	2/4th Bn. Duke Of Wellington's Regt. Order No. 2.	22/04/1917	22/04/1917
Miscellaneous	Instructions		
Miscellaneous	Brigade Carrying Parties		
Heading	War Diary of 2/4 Bn. Duke of Wellingtons Regt. From 1st May To 31st May 1917 Volume 5		
War Diary	Mory Ecoust	02/05/1917	07/05/1917
War Diary	Ervillers	08/05/1917	25/05/1917
Operation(al) Order(s)	2/4th D Of W Regt Operation Order No. 2	22/04/1917	22/04/1917
Miscellaneous	Instructions		
Miscellaneous	Brigade Carrying Parties		
Heading	War Diary of 2/4th Bn. Duke of Wellingtons Regiment From 1st June 1917 To 30th June 1917 Volume No. 6		
War Diary	Achiet Le Petit	17/06/1917	25/06/1917
War Diary	Favreuil Noreuil	27/06/1917	27/06/1917
Heading	War Diary of 2/4th Bn. Duke of Wellingtons Regt. From 1st July 1917 To 31st July 1917 Volume 7		
War Diary	In The Field	01/07/1917	05/07/1917
War Diary	Vaulx	13/07/1917	21/07/1917
War Diary	In The Field	25/07/1917	29/07/1917

Heading	War Diary of 2/4th Bn. Duke of Wellingtons Regiment From 1st August 1917 To 31st August 1917 Volume No. 8		
War Diary	Favreuil	03/08/1917	03/08/1917
War Diary	In The Field	12/08/1917	12/08/1917
War Diary	Favreuil	20/08/1917	20/08/1917
War Diary	In The Field	28/08/1917	28/08/1917
Heading	War Diary of 2/4th Bn. Duke of Wellington's Regt. From 1st September To 30th September 1917. Volume 9		
War Diary	In The Field	06/09/1917	06/09/1917
War Diary	Favreuil	13/09/1917	13/09/1917
War Diary	In The Field	21/09/1917	29/09/1917
Map	Map		
Map	France		
Heading	War Diary of 2/4th Bn Duke of Wellingtons Regt. From 1st October 1917 To:-31st October 1917 (Volume 10)		
War Diary	Favreuil	07/08/1917	07/08/1917
War Diary	In The Field	10/08/1917	12/08/1917
War Diary	Beaulencourt	30/08/1917	30/08/1917
War Diary	Gomiecourt	31/08/1917	31/08/1917
War Diary	Simencourt	31/08/1917	31/08/1917
Heading	2/4 W Riding Regt War Diary Vol 11 Nov 1917		
Miscellaneous	On His Majesty's Service.		
Heading	War Diary of 2/4th Bn, Duke of Wellingtons (WR) Regt. (T.F.) From 1st November 1917 To 30th November 1917 Volume 11		
War Diary	Simencourt	14/11/1917	17/11/1917
War Diary	Achiet-Le-Petit	16/11/1917	16/11/1917
War Diary	Lechelle	18/11/1917	18/11/1917
War Diary	Bertincourt	20/11/1917	21/11/1917
War Diary	Graincourt	21/11/1917	27/11/1917
War Diary	In The Field	28/11/1917	01/12/1917
Miscellaneous	Orders To Be Noted	17/11/1917	17/11/1917
Miscellaneous	2/4th Battalion Instructions	19/11/1917	19/11/1917
Miscellaneous	Tables "B"		
Miscellaneous	Narrative Of Operations	21/11/1917	21/11/1917
Miscellaneous	2 Location Report	20/11/1917	20/11/1917
Miscellaneous	Narrative Of Operations	25/12/1917	25/12/1917
Heading	War Diary of 2/4th Bn. Duke of Wellingtons Regiment From 1st December 1917 To 31st December 1917 Volume 12		
War Diary	In The Field	03/12/1917	03/12/1917
War Diary	Beaumetz	04/12/1917	04/12/1917
War Diary	Bailleulmont	05/12/1917	05/12/1917
War Diary	Montenescourt	06/12/1917	06/12/1917
War Diary	Chelers	10/12/1917	10/12/1917
War Diary	Vendin-Les-Bethune	14/12/1917	14/12/1917
War Diary	L' Ecleme	18/12/1917	18/12/1917
War Diary	Vendin-Les-Bethune	14/12/1917	14/12/1917
War Diary	L' Ecleme	18/12/1917	18/12/1917
War Diary	Vendin-Les-Bethune	19/12/1917	19/12/1917
Heading	War Diary of 2/4th Bn. Duke of Wellingtons (WR) Regt. From 1st January 1918 To 31st January 1918 Volume 13		
War Diary	Chelers	09/08/1918	09/08/1918

War Diary	Maroeuil	13/01/1918	31/01/1918
Operation(al) Order(s)	Bn Order No, 54		
Operation(al) Order(s)	Battalion Order No 55	31/01/1918	31/01/1918
Heading	War Diary of 2/4th Bn. Duke of Wellingtons (WR) Regt. (T.F.) From 1st February 1918 To 28th February 1918 Volume 14		
War Diary	Oppy	01/02/1918	01/02/1918
War Diary	St. Aubin	08/02/1918	08/02/1918
War Diary	Roclincourt	10/02/1918	19/02/1918
Miscellaneous	5th. West Riding Regt Relief Orders By Lt-Col. J. Walker Commanding	05/02/1918	05/02/1918
Operation(al) Order(s)	Battalion Order No. 57	24/02/1918	24/02/1918
Operation(al) Order(s)	Battalion Order No. 57	28/02/1918	28/02/1918
Operation(al) Order(s)	Battalion Order No. 57.	28/02/1918	28/02/1918
Miscellaneous	March Table To Accompany Embussing Instruction		
Miscellaneous	March Table To Accompany Entraining Instructions		
Miscellaneous	2/4th Bn. Duke Of Wellington's Regt.		
Heading	186th Infantry Brigade 62nd Division. 2/4th Battalion Duke Of Wellington's Regiment March 1918		
Heading	War Diary of 2/4th Bn. Duke of Wellington's (WR) Regt (T.F.) From 1st March 1918 To 31st March 1918 Volume 15		
War Diary	Ecoivres	02/03/1918	04/03/1918
War Diary	Ecurie	07/03/1918	07/03/1918
War Diary	In The Line	09/03/1918	09/03/1918
War Diary	Springvale Camp	15/03/1918	15/03/1918
War Diary	Ecurie	15/03/1918	21/03/1918
War Diary	In The Line	22/03/1918	23/03/1918
War Diary	Mount. St. Eloi. Dunsans.	24/03/1918	25/03/1918
War Diary	In The Field	26/03/1918	31/03/1918
Operation(al) Order(s)	Battalion Order No. 59	02/03/1918	02/03/1918
Operation(al) Order(s)	Battalion Order No 62	19/03/1918	19/03/1918
Operation(al) Order(s)	Battalion Order No. 63	20/03/1918	20/03/1918
Operation(al) Order(s)	Battalion Order No. 64	23/03/1918	23/03/1918
Map	Map		
Map	Maroeuil		
Heading	62nd Division. 186th Infantry Brigade 2/4th Battalion The Duke Of Wellington's Regiment April 1918		
Heading	War Diary Of 2/4th Bn. Duke Of Wellingtons (WR) Regt From 1st April 1918 To 30th April 1918 Volume 16		
War Diary	Souastre	02/04/1918	24/04/1918
War Diary	In The Field		
Heading	War Diary of 2/4th. Bn. Duke of Wellingtons (WR) Regt (T.F.) From 1st May 1918 To 31st May 1918 Volume 17		
War Diary	Bois De Warnimont	03/05/1918	24/05/1918
Heading	War Diary of 2/4th Bn. Duke of Wellingtons (WR) Regt. (T.F.) From 1st June 1918 To 30th June 1918 Volume No. 18		
War Diary	In The Field	02/06/1918	02/06/1918
War Diary	In The Field	10/06/1918	24/06/1918
War Diary	Soustare	06/06/1918	06/06/1918
Heading	186th Brigade 62nd Division. 2/4th Bn. Duke Of Wellington's (W.R.) Regt.		

Heading	War Diary of 2/4th Bn. Duke of Wellingtons (WR) Regt (T.F.) From 1st July 1918 To 31st July 1918 Volume No.19		
War Diary	Henu	14/07/1918	31/07/1918
Miscellaneous	Reference Reims S.O.	02/08/1918	02/08/1918
Miscellaneous	2/4 Bn Duke Of Wellington's Regt.	01/07/1918	01/07/1918
Heading	War Diary of 2/4th Bn Duke of Wellingtons (WR) Regt. (T.F.) From 1st August 1918 To 31st August Volume No 20		
War Diary	St. Imoges-Germaine Rd	01/08/1918	01/08/1918
War Diary	Chouilly	04/08/1918	24/08/1918
Miscellaneous	2/4th Bn. Duke Of Wellington's Regiment.	04/09/1918	04/09/1918
Miscellaneous	2/4 Bn Duke Of Wellington's Regt	02/09/1918	02/09/1918
Heading	War Diary Of 2/4 Bn Duke Of Wellington's Regt (T.F.) Volume No. 21		
War Diary	In The Field	02/09/1918	15/09/1918
War Diary	Beugny	16/09/1918	16/09/1918
War Diary	Gomiecourt	25/09/1918	25/09/1918
War Diary	Vaulx-Vraucourt	26/09/1918	26/09/1918
War Diary	Beaumetz	27/09/1918	30/09/1918
Miscellaneous	2/4th Bn. Duke Of Wellington's (W.R.) Regiment	18/09/1918	18/09/1918
Miscellaneous	2/4th Battn. Duke Of Wellington's (W.R.) Regiment 7.7.	01/10/1918	01/10/1918
Miscellaneous	2/4th Bn. Duke Of Wellington's (W.R.) Regiment 1.7.	05/10/1918	05/10/1918
Heading	War Diary Of 2/4th Bn Duke Of Wellington's (W.R.) Regt. October 1918 Volume 22		
War Diary		01/10/1918	31/10/1918
Miscellaneous	2/4th. Battalion Duke Of Wellington's (W.R.) Regiment T.F. Report On Operations-October 8th To 22nd, 1918	08/10/1918	08/10/1918
Miscellaneous	2/4th. Bn. Duke Of Wellington's (W.R.) Regiment, Honours And Award-October, 1918	00/10/1918	00/10/1918
Heading	War Diary Of The 2/4th Duke Of Wellington's Regt November 1918 Volume No 23		
War Diary		01/11/1918	30/11/1918
Miscellaneous	2/4th Bn. Duke Of Wellington's Regiment.	11/11/1918	11/11/1918
Miscellaneous	Honours And Awards-November, 1918.	02/12/1918	02/12/1918
Heading	War Diary Of 2/4th Battn. Duke Of Wellington's Volume No. 24 December 1918		
War Diary	Conjoux	01/12/1918	06/12/1918
War Diary	Leignon	07/12/1918	10/12/1918
War Diary	Failon	11/12/1918	11/12/1918
War Diary	Ocquier	12/12/1918	12/12/1918
War Diary	Hoopet	13/12/1918	13/12/1918
War Diary	Rahier	14/12/1918	14/12/1918
War Diary	Petit Halleux	16/12/1918	16/12/1918
War Diary	Ville Du Bois	17/12/1918	17/12/1918
War Diary	Deidenburg	22/12/1918	22/12/1918
War Diary	Bullingen	23/12/1918	23/12/1918
War Diary	Hollerath	24/12/1918	24/12/1918
War Diary	Sotenich	25/12/1918	25/12/1918
War Diary	Roggendorf	25/12/1918	25/12/1918
Miscellaneous	2/4th Battn. Duke Of Wellington's Regiment.	00/12/1918	00/12/1918
Heading	2/4 Duke Of Wellington's (W.R.) Regiment (T.F.) War Diary 1st To 31st January 1919 Volume XXI		
War Diary	Roggendorf	01/01/1919	31/01/1919
War Diary	Germany	01/01/1919	31/01/1919

Miscellaneous	2/4 Bn Duke Of Wellington's (W.R.) Regt (T.F.) Appendix No 1	16/01/1919	16/01/1919
Heading	War Diary of The 2/4 Bn Duke Of Wellington's (W.R.) Regiment (T.F.) From 1st February 1919 To 28th February 1918 Vol 26		
War Diary	Roggendorf Germany	01/02/1919	21/02/1919
War Diary	Bulpech Germany	22/02/1919	28/02/1919
Miscellaneous	2/4th Bn. Duke of Wellington's (W.R.) Regt. Honours and Awards-February Appendix 1		

ma05/3086(1)

ma05/3086(1)

62ND DIVISION
186TH INFY BDE

2-4TH BN DUKE OF WELLINGTON'S REGT

JAN 1917-DEC 1918

1919 FEB

TO 6 DIV / MIDLAND BDE

62ND DIVISION
186TH INFY BDE

ORIGINAL   Vol 1

Confidential

War Diary

of

2/4th Bn Duke of Wellington's Regt.

from 9th January 1917 to 31st January 1917 (incl.)

Volume 1

WAR DIARY
or
INTELLIGENCE SUMMARY

(Erase heading not required.)

Army Form C. 2118

7th Duke of Wellington's Regt

Instructions regarding War Diaries and Intelligence Summaries are contained in F.S. Regs., Part II. and the Staff Manual respectively. Title Pages will be prepared in manuscript.

Place	Date	Hour	Summary of Events and Information	Remarks and references to Appendices
Southampton	Jan 9		The Batt arrived in Southampton, the right half Batt under Col H.E.P. Nash stayed the night at the rest camp, the left half Batt under Major St Kenney crossed to Havre. The Transport went with the Capt Half Batt.	J.S.L.
	10th		The ½ right half Batt crossed to Havre on the "Duchess of Argyll" & proceeded to the rest camp, where it joined to left half Batt.	J.S.L.
Havre	11th		The Batt entrained for Aire - a - Chalons.	J.S.L.
	12th		The Batt arrived at Aire - a - Chalons & marched to Villers ? Hospital, J.S.L. where it went into billets.	J.S.L.
	13th		Received 3 Barr & Stroud Range Finders & Tangent sights at Havre.	J.S.L.
Villers Hospital	15th		Rigifers Gloves received for the Batt.	J.S.L.
	17th		Leather Jerkins received for the Batt.	J.S.L.
	22nd		The Batt marched to Amplier & spent the night in tents.	J.S.L.
	23rd		The Batt marched to Bus les Artois & went into a British Camp.	
Bus	28th		Officers & O.R. finished instruction in the Trenches. ?/S.L.	J.S.L.
	31st		Officers & O.R. finished instruction in the Trenches.	J.S.L.
	25th		Received bugles for Buglers from Ordnance at Bus.	J.S.L.

A.S. Nowell Lt Col
216 D. O. W. Regt

WAR DIARY or INTELLIGENCE SUMMARY

Army Form C. 2118

2/4 Bn. of Wellington Regt.

Place	Date	Hour	Summary of Events and Information	Remarks and references to Appendices
Eno	Jan. 26		Received 16 trench Helios, 1 Kibball test Shoemakers filled, 8 covers Lewis Gun, 8 thing Lewis Gun from Ordnance at Eno.	J.A.E.
	27th		Received 4 Lewis Guns complete, 22 trays Magazine, 44 Carriers Mag. as per W.6 Mag. equip. & Machine Munting, 150 Carriers Hand Grenade, 500 stokes Cleaning Chambers from Ordnance at Eno.	J.A.E.
	28th		Received 4 Telescopic rifles, 3 Pannier Signalling, 19 Cope Machinist, 48 Stone Help, Pairs, 1 Rifle Sent R.L.E. III * from Ordnance at Eno.	J.A.E. J.A.E.
	29th		Received 25 Periscopes No 9 & 80 Periscopes Vigilant from Ordnance Eno.	J.A.E.
	30th		Capt H. A. Kerkum. R.A.M.C evacuated to base hospital.	J.A.E.
	31st		J. Young M. 35º Officers (including) 966 O.R. M.O. attached	

H. E. Sharp Lt Col
2/4 6 T 6 Regt.

Original

Confidential

Vol 2

War Diary

of

2/4th Bn. Duke of Wellington's Regt.

From 1st February 1917 to 28th February 1917 (incl.)

Volume II

WAR DIARY or INTELLIGENCE SUMMARY

Army Form C. 2118

Original

2/4 Sqdn of Welsh Fd Coy

Place	Date	Hour	Summary of Events and Information	Remarks and references to Appendices
Busa	Feb. 2.		Received Box Respirators No 3. 860. No 2, 120. No.m. 110. from Ordnance Stores.	J.S.L.
	3.		Sgt A. E. Priestley sent to hospital. 2/2 Field Ambulance (A.R.).	J.S.L.
	3.		Received 32 Body Shields, 32 Rockets, 1 Lamp Bengal Ambrosine Signal	J.S.L.
	3.		A. e. 15 Coys went into the trenches for 24 hrs. another instruction & went attached to the 5-6th Bde 19th Div. Bayonet, 2/15 th to 5-6th Sec 19 Div. The Sgt Received 4 Pistols Signal 12" No1 M.K.I from Ordnance Stores.	J.S.L. J.17.2.
	3.		C & D Coys went into the trenches for 24 hrs under instruction, R & G were attached to the 5-6th Bde 19th Div. Bayonet 0 D Coy to the 58th Bde 19Div. The Sgt	J.S.L. J.17.2.
	4.		Received 34 Cups Tommy. 2 Lewis Guns complete, 8 Box Tin Magazines. 16 Carriers Canvas, 64 Magazines, from Ordnance Stores	J.S.L.
	6.		Lt. D.A.S. Killew & 18 O.R. proceeded to Auchenbreck to form party of The Brigade Mining Section. Lt. D.A.S. Killew was placed in charge.	J.S.L.
	8.		Major S.P. Lacey & Capt D.A. Latreille & 16 OR went to the Trenches for instruction for 48 hrs. They were attached to the 32 Inf Div. In 2nd Brigade.	J.S.L.
	9.		Four Officers & 54 O.R. proceeded to the trenches in advance of the Batt'.	J.S.L.
	12.		Capt 'C' Clarkson O.C. D. Co. died of Generalised Septicaemia while on a course of instruction at the I Army School	CRSS

H. H. Hartley Lt Col
CO 68 2/4 2/17 W. Welsh Regt

WAR DIARY or INTELLIGENCE SUMMARY

Army Form C. 2118

Place	Date	Hour	Summary of Events and Information	Remarks and references to Appendices
Bus	Feb 13		The batⁿ moved to the trenches & held the line K.35 to K.44. 48 to the junction of Flag Avenue & trench French (See trench map Helebrine 57d. S.W.) Batⁿ. H.Q. was at White City Q.11.A.6.2. A + C Companies in line, B + D in support. Capt. W. Graham reported for duty & took command of D. Co. Capt. J. A. Ellison sent down the line sick.	PSS
trenches	Feb 15		On the night of 14 & 15th B + D companies went into the line. A + C in support. Lt H. Sinclair + 1 man killed. 5 others were wounded.	PSS
	16			PSS
	17		The batⁿ was relieved by the 2/4th D of W Inf^y & went into billets in Mailly Maillet. All available men employed on Corps Working Parties.	PSS
Mailly Maillet	21		The batⁿ moved to a camp (huts + tents) in Mailly Wood East.	PSS
	25		At 4.40 AM orders were received to be prepared to move by 5.30 AM (with remainder of Brigade) to support the 187th Bde who were feeling out towards BEAREGARD DOVECOTE + PUISIEUX.	PSS

WAR DIARY or INTELLIGENCE SUMMARY

Army Form C. 2118

Place	Date	Hour	Summary of Events and Information	Remarks and references to Appendices
Mailly Wood E	4th 25		The batt? stood fast all day awaiting orders.	RSS
	26	3 AM	A draft of 16 other ranks arrived from 34th I.B.D. ETAPLES. Operation Orders received at 8.30 P.M. Batt? to occupy dug-outs south of BEAUMONT HAMEL pending further orders. Batt? H.Q. to be at Q.17.a.8.8. Sheet 57d S.E.	RSS
	27		Batt? moved to new position. H.Q. at Q.17.a.8.8. A & B Companies Q.16.d.1.6. C & D Companies Q.11.d central. (Sheet 57 D S.E.)	RSS
		2 PM	Orders received to move immediately to R.1.d.7.6 (Sheet 57d S.E.) Move completed by 4.30 P.M.	
	28		Batt? in reserve to the 2/5th & 2/6th Dukes of Wellington Regt. Batt? moved to a rest camp at Q.11.d.3.5. (Sheet 57d S.E.)	RSS
		5.15 PM	2/Lt T.H. Linton reported for duty & was posted to "B" Co. During the past 3 days rations & water were conveyed to the Batt? on pack mules. This was necessary owing to the extremely muddy condition of the roads.	RSS

H.D. Hartley Lt Col
Comdg 2/4 Bn 7 W Reg?

Confidential

War Diary of Vol 3

2/4th Bn. Duke of Wellington's Reg.

from 1st March 1917 to 31st March 1917

Volume 3

WAR DIARY / INTELLIGENCE SUMMARY

Army Form C. 2118

2/4th Bn Duke of Wellington's Regt

Place	Date	Hour	Summary of Events and Information	Remarks and references to Appendices
Y RAVINE BEAUMONT HAMEL	1918 Mch 1st		Coys Working Parties supplied for the making of roads. All available men taken.	R.U.
	4		Batt. moved into billets at FORCEVILLE	R.U.
Forceville	6		The attack was practised on ground resembling that at ACHIET-LE-PETIT.	R.U.
	14		Batt. moved into Quarry Dugout Station Rd Beaumont Hamel. 2/Lt J.H. Lister & eight men wounded while on a working party on the Essex Railway.	J.S.L.
Beaumont Hamel	15		The Batt. moved into the line, relieving the 2/6 along the Monument— Achiet-le-Puisieux Railway from G.9.D.9.6 to G.15.D.1.3, Ref Map 57c29, relieving two Battalions, one of the Northumberland Fusiliers & the 2/5 Yorkshire Light Infantry. On firing to the trenches some of the companies were very heavily shelled. B Coy losing 9 men wounded. The Batt. held the Railway line in the embankment. 110 Chgwts or Trenches.	J.S.L. J.S.L. J.S.L.
In the Field	16		During the day & the 16th the enemy shelled heavily the railway embankment & the East enemy casualties 2 killed & 13 wounded. At midnight a fighting patrol was pushed out from 2nd Corpmy, to reconnoitre & if possible establish a line along the enemy front from G.20.A.8.7. to G.15.C.6.8. East Patrol consisted of 1 Officer & twelve other ranks.	J.S.L.

WAR DIARY or INTELLIGENCE SUMMARY

Army Form C. 2118

Place	Date	Hour	Summary of Events and Information	Remarks and references to Appendices
In the Field	Nov 17th		Sent a team of 12 riflemen at 3 A.M. this time was established by J.A.S. without casualties to ascertain the enemy's new line. At 3.30 A.M. Lieut. Loney by took a similar patrol into the village of Achiet-le-Petit, & found the enemy had just left the village. By this time our new line had been reinforced from the railway entrenchment. The left of our line pushed forward through the village & was established along the SUNKEN Rd. from Q.5.C.5.4. to Q.15.D.1.4, our new line (with A, B, & half D Coys. in the front line & the Ref Map 70.39). With A, B & half D Coys. in the front line & the remainder of D Coy in support in the trenches at the southern entrance to the village. Patrols were pushed out from 'A' Coy on the left, on the railway and as far as Longford on a J.A.S. about the railway and as far as Longford on a and the right of the railway and also at the other company at Q.15.D.1.4. Another forward Achiet-le-Grand. Both Patrols reached the BIHUCOURT LINE without resistance & finding the trenches unoccupied to a distance of about 300 yds east side of the railway. The patrols pushed forward into Achiet-le-Grand which was worked at 2.15 P.M. at Q.16.a.4.9 (Map 7039) Yet — another patrol came into heavy artillery & machine gun fire, sustaining four casualties 2 killed & 2 wounded. After annihilation J.S.R. the sulfonate who occupied a line on the north & west part of the village, our two patrols took up a position on the west of the village, one patrol in the brickworks & the other at Bruges Q.10.C.3.9 (Map 7039)	

WAR DIARY
or
INTELLIGENCE SUMMARY

(Erase heading not required.)

Army Form C. 2118

Instructions regarding War Diaries and Intelligence Summaries are contained in F.S. Regs., Part II. and the Staff Manual respectively. Title Pages will be prepared in manuscript.

Place	Date	Hour	Summary of Events and Information	Remarks and references to Appendices
In the Field	17th		A working party of 300/400 men under J.A.S. who were observed to be digging in about 1000 yds advance from G.4 a.7.3. to G.4.S.7.2 (approx), were attacked by our 18 pdr gunners. These two patrols were withdrawn on the afternoon of the 18th. Its time taken over by the 45 spent holding the line of G.12.D Cap/also pointed sapper partie by which its digging this during the day. 6 killed 76 wounded. 17th were 5 killed, 27 wounded [?]	J.A.S.
	18th		Batt. HdQrs were established at G.13. 5.6.5 (approx) at 3pm on the 17th inst. On the afternoon of the 18th a Coy ths patrols were withdrawn from the village of Achiet-le-Grand to the SUNKEN Rd. The Batt. being then in support to the 4/5- Scots heavy bns.	J.A.S. J.A.S.
	19th		The Batt. N.R.S. occupied billets in Achiet-le-Petit.	
	11th		Received bayo rifle covers 250. Guns Lewis Empts 2. Brass carriers Mag. Zn 8. Carriers Magazine 16. Magazines 64.	
	12th		Received Bayo rifle Covers 730.	J.A.S.
	26th		Received Sights Luminous No.I R.I.F. Sets. 64.	J.A.S.

A.R. Stewart
Lt Col
2/4 D.C.L.I. Regt.

ORIGINAL Vol 4

Confidential

War diary of

2/4th Bn. Duke of Wellington's Reg"

from 1st April 1917 to 30th April 1917

Volume 4

WAR DIARY or INTELLIGENCE SUMMARY

Army Form C. 2118

Place	Date	Hour	Summary of Events and Information	Remarks and references to Appendices
Achiet-le-Petit	6/6		The Battn moved to ERVILLERS.	J.S.L.
Ervillers	8th		Received 8 Pistols, holsters & 8 Ports Cleaning Pls from Ordnance. Also 32 Patches distinguishing for Signallers.	J.S.L.
Ervillers	10th		The Battn moved to MORY, but subsequently 2 Coys returned to ERVILLERS.	J.S.L.
Ervillers	11th		The Battn at ERVILLERS moved to MORY.	J.S.L.
Mory	12th		The 2 Coys at ERVILLERS moved into the line in support of the 9/Dffs. Rgt. 2 Coys & HdQrs were stationed in ECOUST & 2 Coys were stationed about 1324 & 9.9. (Ref: Sheet 57c NW, 1:20:000 SA)	J.S.L.
			Received 6 from a Signalling Course from Ordnance.	J.S.L.
Ecoust	13th		Casualties. 1 killed 8 wounded Other Ranks	J.S.L.
	14th		Casualties. 3 Other ranks wounded. 4 of which accidentally.	J.S.L.
	15th		Major R.G. Buchanan reported for duty, & took over the duties of 2nd in command.	J.S.L.
			The following officers reinforcements reported. 2/Lt. J. H. Brown, 2/Lt. R.R. Coper, 2/Lt. F. Ashcroft, 2/Lt. G.T. Robertson.	J.S.L.
			Casualties. 7 killed 12 wounded, Other Ranks.	J.S.L.
	16th		Casualties. 1 killed 0 10 wounded, Other Ranks.	J.S.L.
	17th		Lt. J. Mackibbin killed. 2/Lt. S.H. Mavesie wounded. O.H wounded Other Ranks. The Battn came out of the line, having been relieved by the 22nd Manchester,	J.S.L.
			Came back into MORY.	
			The Padre, Officer Mourigné, left the unit & reported from the base hospital than Ervillers.	J.S.L.

WAR DIARY
or
INTELLIGENCE SUMMARY

Army Form C. 2118

Place	Date	Hour	Summary of Events and Information	Remarks and references to Appendices
Ervaut	April 13/4		2/Lt L Cowdrey by & 15 other ranks exploded at Bangalore Torpedoes in the trenches nine in front of BULLECOURT	J.S.L.
MORY.	19		The Battn moved from MORY to B 26 central (approx) (At Shut 57 NW Ed 5A)	J.S.L.
B26 central 20			Casualties. 2 other Ranks wounded whilst carrying stores into Ervaut.	J.S.L.

J.E. Sharbolol
2/Lt A&W Regt.
(Cont)

2/4th Bn. Duke of Wellington's Regt.   Order No. 2.

22.4.17.

Reference } BULLECOURT Edn. 2 A 1/10.000.
Maps.   } Sheet 57.C. N.W. 1/20.000.

1. (a) 62nd Division will attack HINDENBURG LINE.
   4th Australian Division will be attacking simultaneously on our RIGHT
   7th Division will be holding line on LEFT of 62nd Division but will not attack.
   (b) 185th Brigade, less 1 Battn. is responsible for capture of BULLECOURT.

2. Boundaries of 62nd Division are as shown on attached map.

3. (a) Objectives will be as under:-
   1st Line of HINDENBURG TRENCH, U.20.b - U.21.a, b, + d - U.22.c.
   2nd German Trench - U.15.a.5.6. - U.15.d - U.15.c, and line of roadway
   U.16.c. 4.5. - U.22.b.8.5.
   3rd HENDECOURT, and line U.15.a.5.6. - U.9.d.2.4. - U.11.b.8.0. -
   U.12.c.7.7.
   (b) Attack will be carried out simultaneously by 185th on RIGHT -
   186th in CENTRE - 187th on LEFT.
   (c) RIGHT Boundary of 186th will be line U.27.a.6.7. - Cross Roads U.27.b.15.80.
   - junction of Road and Trench U.21.d.5.6.
   From here responsibility of 186th extends to roadway at U.22.d.0.2. -
   U.22.b.8.5. - thence line EAST of HENDECOURT and CHATEAU and WOOD
   in U.12.c. -
   LEFT Boundary of 186th will be line Cross Roads U.20.d.9.4. -
   junction of Road and Trench U.21.a.5.1. - thence line through
   U.16.a.0.0. to U.10.b.5.0.

4. (a) Forming up line for leading waves of 186th will be line of roadway
   U.27.a.6.7. - U.20.d.9.4.
   (b) Taped lines will only be laid for leading wave of each Battn. of
   Brigade.

5. (a) Attack on 1st Objective will be carried out by 2/5th on RIGHT and
   2/6th on LEFT.
   (b) Attack on 2nd and 3rd Objectives will be carried out by 2/7th on
   RIGHT and 2/4th on LEFT
   (c) 3 Coys. of 2/8th WEST YORKS. Regt. will take over line of 2nd
   objective after capture from 2/7th + 2/4th prior to ZERO plus 2 hours
   2/7th + 2/4th will then advance on 3rd objective.

6. Dividing line between Battalions will be line from U.21.c.4.1. -
   U.21.b.15.05. thence Trench junction U.22.a.65.95. - Roadway
   U.17.a.20.35. - Road junction U.17.a.45.90. - Road junction at
   U.11.b.2.3. (all inclusive to 2/7th)

7. (a) 2/4th will form up 20 yards in rear of 2/6th in artillery formation
   'B' Coy on RIGHT and 'D' Coy. on LEFT will form 1st + 2nd waves.
   'A' "   "   "   "   "   'C'   "   "   "   "   " 3rd + 4th "
   (b) Dividing line between Coys. will be line from U.21.c.15.25. -
   U.21.b.0.3. - Trench junction U.15.d.95.40. - Trench junction
   at U.16.c.10.45. - junction Road and Trench U.16.c.9.6. (all
   above inclusive to 'D' Coy) - thence to Cross Roads V.11.c.0.4.
   (inclusive to 'C' Coy.) - thence to U.11.a.25.00 -
   (c) At ZERO plus 1 hour and 15 minutes, 2/7th and 2/4th will have
   formed up EAST of 1st objective, and will move forward in
   extended order keeping up close under barrage, to line of 2nd

objective.

The 1st and 2nd waves will be responsible for capture of 2nd objective.

1st and 2nd wave of 'B' and 'D' Coys. will advance to Trench U.16.c. - U.15.d.

They will be responsible for mopping up this trench.

3rd and 4th waves will pass through 1st and 2nd waves and form up EAST of 2nd objective under barrage, in readiness for subsequent advance on 3rd objective.

These two Coys. 'A' and 'C', will then form 1st and 2nd waves of Battn., 'B' and 'D' Coys. becoming 3rd and 4th waves.

Advance on 3rd objective will be commenced at ZERO plus 2 hours and 5 minutes, at which hour barrage will lift.

8. Touch must be established and maintained throughout whole advance with units on RIGHT and LEFT flanks.

9. (a) Rate of advance is governed by barrage time table as shown on attached map, and is at rate of 2 minutes per 100 yards.

(b) The importance of keeping as close as possible on heels of barrage must be most strongly impressed on all ranks.

(c) All Officers and NCOs must keep in line with their platoons or sections and not move in advance or in rear of them.

(d) O.C. Coys. are reminded that on reaching line U.17.c.2.9. - U.10.c.7.0. the barrage commences to swing forward on LEFT, while remaining stationary on RIGHT. This will necessitate RIGHT Coys. almost halting while LEFT Coys. move forward.

O.C. Coys. must be most careful not to lose direction owing to swinging barrage.

10. (a) After capture of 3rd objective 'A' and 'C' Coys. will establish at least two strong points per Coy. front, to hold one Lewis Gun detachment and twelve riflemen.

(b) In addition to above strong points will be constructed and garrisoned with same force as follows:-

'B' Coy. at U.11.d.4.6.

'D' Coy. at EAST end of CEMETARY - U.10.d.7.7.

(c) After capture of 3rd objective Major LEAROID will go forward and take command of line thus established. He will be responsible for supervising general work of consolidation and that Lewis Guns are sited in best possible positions.

(d) After capture of 3rd objective O.C. 'B' and 'D' Coys will select suitable positions in support of 'A' and 'C' Coys. respectively.

O.C. 'B' Coy. is responsible for clearing and mopping up houses, cellars, and dugouts on road in HENDECOURT from U.17.a.9.5. - to U.11.c.2.3.

11. Attack will be supported by M.G.'s of 218th M.G. Coy. and when final objective has been gained, these guns will be located at following strong points:-

(a) Factory - U.22.b.1.7. 2 guns.
(b) Roadway. U.17.a.8.0. 1 gun
(c) Road Junction U.17.b.3.6. 1 gun.

12. 6 Tanks will assist in operations and in capture of 2nd objective.

They will follow Infantry as closely as possible but Infantry will not wait for Tanks.

13. 15th Sqdn. R.F.C. will provide contact aeroplanes to patrol during operations.
These aeroplanes will demand information from Infantry by signals on KLAXON horns or by dropping white lights. Infantry will light red flares or wave their helmets in order to shew their whereabouts.

14. Runner Relay Posts will be established at following points:-
   (a) Road junction   U. 27. b. 2. 9.   4 Runners.
   (b) Factory   U. 22. b. 0. 7.   8 Runners.
   (c) Road junction   U. 17. a. 5. 2.   4 Runners.

2/Lieut. CORDINGLEY will establish these posts as advance progresses.

15. (a) Report Centres will be as under:-
   Advanced Brigade Report Centre   B. 6. d. 4. 5.
   Battn.   "   "   "
   Aid Post   U. 26. C. 8. 0. (Rly. Embankment)
                                   U. 26. C. 8. 0. ("   )

   (b) As soon as 2nd objective has been gained, Lieut FLETCHER with telephone will move forward and select a site for Battn. Hd Qrs. in 1st objective.
   Similarly on 3rd objective being attained he will select a site in 2nd objective.
   These sites will be as near as possible to line of Relay Posts.

16. (a) All Coy. H.Q. established in any captured dugouts cellars etc will have a sentry posted at entrance to direct orderlies bringing messages and to give alarm in case of counter attack.
    (b) On establishment they will inform Battn. H.Q. of their whereabouts, giving coordinates.
    (c) Coy. runners must be informed of positions of Battn. and all Coy. H.Q.

17. On outer flanks of Coys. forming leading waves there will be 1 officer and 1 NCO whose sole duty it is to maintain direction.
They will all be provided with compasses and will know the bearing for the advance.

J.B. Ellison
Capt & Adjt
2/4 B.

Copy No I   to A Coy
Copy No II   B Coy
do   No III C Coy
do   No IV   D Coy
do   No V   2nd i/c
do   No VI   S.O.
do   No VII Int. Off
do   No VIII C.O.
do   No IX   Adjutant
do   No X   War Diary
do   No XI   Spare
do   No XII War Diary

Instructions

Rations. All ranks will carry unexpended portion of the day's rations, the iron ration, and a second iron ration. The iron ration will not be consumed without the O.C.'s sanction.

Hot Meal. O.C. Coys. and Hd. Qr. Coy. will see that a hot meal is given to troops as late as possible. Cookers only can be used.

Water. All bottles will be carried filled.

Rum. A rum ration will be issued to Battalions as late as possible.

S.A.A. and Grenades. The Brigade dump is at C.2.b.1.8.

Stores to be carried.

- **Mills Grenades.** Every man will carry not 2 bombs in breast pocket (Battn. Runners and Battn. Signallers excepted)
- **Mills Grenades.** 8 per bomber in bandoliers
- **Rifle Grenades.** 8 per rifle bomber in buckets.
- **Sandbags.** 2 per man, rolled and fastened to braces.
- **Flares.** 1 per man, in side pocket.
- **Wire cutters and Gloves.** 10 per Coy. - selected men - fastened in belt.
- **Very Pistols.** 1 for each Officer and Platoon Commanders of 'A' and 'C' Coys. - remainder with Officers of 'B' and 'D' Coys. Two men will be detailed to accompany each Officer or Platoon NCO carrying a very pistol, to carry 6 red and 12 green lights each.
  O.C. Coys. will, when consolidating, see that every strong post has a very pistol and lights.
- **P. Bombs.** Carried by every Officer NCO and men of bombing sections.
- **Shovels and Picks.** 'A' + 'C' Coys. 30 shovels 10 picks each } to be carried by rearwaves of each Coy.
  'B' + 'D' Coys. 20 shovels 10 picks each }
- **Platoon Flags.** 1 per platoon.
- **Wire Breakers.** All available will be carried.
- **Field Dressing and Ampule.** By every man.
- **S.O.S. Signals.** 1 green, 1 red, 1 green flare or rocket. Our Artillery will open fire on seeing a green and red rocket or light.
- **Code Names.** In sending messages code names will not be used.
- **Papers etc.** No secret map, tracing or documents of any value of military information will be taken into the attack.
- **Dug outs.** All captured dug outs will be systematically searched by special patrols - an Officer will be in charge, and should be accompanied by a medical orderly.

Brigade Carrying Parties.

Strength	Duty	Report to	Time
⊙ 1 Officer	Carrying to	Capt: Bruce at	Zero minus
+ 2 NCOs	Advanced	Brigade Dump	2 hours.
+ 25 O.R.	Battn. Dump.	C.2.b.1.8.	
✱ 2 Runners.	Between Bde. and Advanced Bn. Dump.	do	do.

⊙ 2/Lt. Lister.
+ 1 NCO 13 men 'B' Coy.
+ 1 NCO 12 men 'D' "
✱ 1 man 'B'.
✱ 1 man 'D'.

Battalion Carrying Parties.

Matts - 20 'B' Coy.
20 'D' " } Will be issued at Brigade Dump C.2.b.1.8.

They will be carried by men of the leading waves as far as the 1st objective.

French Bridge - 1 per Coy. - will be issued at Bde. Dump C.2.b.1.8. To be carried as far as the 1st objective.

Company Carrying Parties.

Party of 1 NCO and 10 men to carry:-
  2 bundles shovels - 2 men
  40 bandoliers SAA - 4 men } will be issued at Bde. Dump C.2.b.1.8.
  8 box bombs - 4 men

These parties will follow rear waves of the Battn.
O.C. Coys. will ensure that NCOs know beforehand position of Brigade Dump.

Officers and NCOs in charge of carrying parties will have with them list of names and regt: numbers of the men of their parties. Yellow bands will be worn.

The advanced Battn. Dump will be established on the western edge of wood, west of Hendecourt V.16.c.9.6.

Liaison. Sgt. Gibson will report to the Hd. Qrs. of the right Battn. of the 187th Bde. at Zero minus 2 hours.

Dress. Fighting Order. Haversack on back with waterproof sheet rolled on top. Jerkins will be worn under the coat.

Prisoners. Escort at rate of 2 men per 10 prisoners. Prisoners will only be searched for arms. Officers will be searched for papers at once. All prisoners will be sent to Bde. Dump, and receipts obtained.

Packs & Battn. Property. will be dumped at Qm. Stores on afternoon.

Entrenching Tools. will not be carried by runners, Signallers, carrying parties, Sergeants.

Police. Sgt. Danby, Ptes. Kenyon, Knapton, Mundy, will be responsible for the collection and conducting to Divisional Stragglers Station any stragglers detained at Road junction at ERVILLERS at B.13.b.2.9. The Stragglers Station is at Behagnies H.2.a.5.9.

J.B. Ellison
Capt & Adjt.
2/4 K.

Confidential

War diary

of

2/4 Bn. Duke of Wellingtons Reg^t

from 1st May to 31st May 1917

Volume 5

WEST RIDING

WAR DIARY
INTELLIGENCE SUMMARY

Army Form C. 2118.

1/4 Duke of Wellington's Regt.

Place	Date	Hour	Summary of Events and Information	Remarks and references to Appendices
MORY	1917 May 2nd		The Batt'n moved into the line on the Railway Embankment North of ECOUST.	/A.S.E.
ECOUST	3rd	3.45am	The Batt'n attacked the HINDENBURG LINE in conjunction with the remainder of the Division, the objectives being as shown in "Operation Orders" attached.	1
		5.30am	The first attack was not successful & a party of 4 Officers & 90 men who had retired to the Embankment were led forward by Capt H.N. WALLER in a second attempt; at 6.15am this party were again forced back having had very heavy casualties. During the operation the following Officers were killed, wounded & missing. Killed. Capt W. Graham. 2/Lt A.E. Priestley. Missing. 2/Lt O.R.A. Appleton. 2/Lt G.H. Pickett. Wounded. 2/Lt H. Arnett. 2/Lt T.J. Roberts. 2/Lt J.H. Lister. 2/Lt J.S. Meadows. Other Ranks. Killed 7. Wounded 154. Missing. 72.	
			The Batt'n held the Embankment with 2 Officers & 150 O.R. from O.26.c.20.05 to C.2.t.1.9. until the night of May 4/5th, the Remainder of the Batt'n returning to MORY.	/A.S.E.

WAR DIARY or INTELLIGENCE SUMMARY

Army Form C. 2118.

1/4 Bn. of Wellington Regt.

Place	Date	Hour	Summary of Events and Information	Remarks and references to Appendices
MORY	1917 May 4th & May 5th		The Battn. moved to MORY COPSE in support of the line. In the morning of May 5/17 between the Battalions brought in information as to the whereabouts of 4 of the R.E. miners who were lying out wounded. Lt. Butterworth though wounded himself volunteered to guide a party to the R.E. wounded. According to the orders of Lt. Col. May, Lt. Col. Loughton, Lt. Butterworth & other parties went out, but were not successful in recovering any wounded but 3 other shelter cases were brought in.	J.S.L. J.S.L.
	6th		On the 6th May the Battn. moved into the line on the Railway Embankment North of ECOUST, relieving the 2/6 Depots of the 2/7 Depot Rgt. Casualties Other Ranks 1 killed 7 wounded.	J.S.L.
	7th		Lt. A.S. Loughton again made an attempt to recover the R.E. miners & was successful, & he also brought back information which led to the rescue of 33 Other Ranks, who were lying out wounded.	J.S.L.
	8th		The Battn. was relieved by the 2/7 West Yorks Rgt. & went into Camp at ERVILLERS.	J.S.L.

Army Form C. 2118.

WAR DIARY
or
INTELLIGENCE SUMMARY.
(Erase heading not required.)

2/4th Duke of Wellington's Regt

Place	Date	Hour	Summary of Events and Information	Remarks and references to Appendices
ERVILLERS	1917 May 6		Received 1 Limbered wagon G.S. from Ordnance	J.A.C.
	9th		Received 5 Lewis Guns complete, from Ordnance	J.A.C.
	11th		Received 2 Telescopic Rifles H.L.E. from Ordnance	J.A.C.
	12th		The Batt. went into the line. Strengthened by 2 Coys of the 2/6th & 2/5th Bs 2/5 S.L. Relieving the line from U.28.C.6.2. to T.2 & T.1.3. Map Sheet 51B S.W.	J.S.L.
	16th		Received 2 Lewis Guns complete from Ordnance	J.A.C.
	20th		The Batt. were relieved in the line by 2/5 K.O.Y.L.I. & went into billets at Courcelles. Casualties Other Ranks. 3 killed 1 missing 14 wounded.	J.S.L.
	17th		The Batt. took 7 German prisoners	J.S.L.
	25		Received 118 Carriers Magazine from Ordnance	J.S.L.

Buchanan Major
p.p. O.C. 2/4 Duke of Wellington's Regt

Appendix 1   Copy No. 10 Windsor

2/4th D of W Regt
Operation Order No 2 (amended)

Ref. Maps   BULLECOURT Edn. 2a 1/10,000
             Sheet 57c N.W.   1/20,000
             HENDECOURT   1/50,000

Battn. Operation Order No 2 d/d 22.4.17 is cancelled and following substituted :-

1. (a)   62nd Divn. will attack HINDENBURG LINE
         2nd Austr. Divn. will be attacking simultaneously on our right
         7th Divn. will be holding line on left of 62nd Div. but will not attack
   (b)   185 Bde. (less 1 Bn.) is responsible for the capture of BULLECOURT

2.   Boundaries of 62 Divn. are as shown on attached map

3. (a)   Objectives will be as under :-
         1st — line of HINDENBURG TRENCH   U.20.b. - U.21.a.v.d - U.22.c.
         2nd   GERMAN TRENCH - U.15.a.5.b. - U.15.d - U.3.c.
         and line of roadway U.16.c.4.5. - U.22.b.8.5.
         3rd   HENDECOURT and line U.15.a.5.b. - U.9.d.2.4 - U.11.b.8.0 - U.12.c.7.7.
   (b)   Attack will be carried out simultaneously by 185th on RIGHT 186th in CENTRE and 187th on LEFT
   (c)   RIGHT BOUNDARY of 186th will be line U.27.a.6.7 - cross roads U.27.b.15.80 - junction of Road and Trench U.21.d.5.6. From here responsibility of 186th extends to

Roadway at U.22.d.0.2. - U.22.b.8.5 - thence line EAST of HENDECOURT, CHATEAU and WOOD in U.12.c.
LEFT BOUNDARY of 183rd will be line Cross Roads U.20.d.9.4. - Junction of road and Trench U.21.a.5.1 - thence line through U.16.a.0.0. to U.10.b.5.0.

4. (a) Forming up line for leading waves of 186th will be line of U.26.d.9.9 - U.26.b.30.65 ~~roadway thro~~ ~~at Jap~~ ~~embankment~~ ~~Road~~.

(b) Taped lines will only be laid for leading wave of each Bn. of Bde. There will be posts with square Boards on top marking 2/4th flanks. } Taped lines will be run to mark RIGHT and LEFT flanks of 186th. The latter from U.26.b.30.65. (left of forming up line leading waves of 2/6th) to crossroads U.20.d.9.4.

5. (a) Attack on 1st objective will be carried out by 2/5th on RIGHT and 2/6th on LEFT.

(b) Attack on 2nd and 3rd will be carried out by 2/7th on RIGHT and 2/4th on LEFT.

(c) 3 Coys of 2/8th WEST YORKS will take over line of 2nd objective after capture, from 2/7th and 2/4th prior to ZERO plus 2 hours.
2/7th and 2/4th will then continue advance on 3rd objective

6. Dividing line between Bns will be line from U.21.c.4.1. - U.26.a.3.9. - U.21.b.15.05. thence Trench Junction U.22.a.65.95. - Roadway U.17.a.20.35 - Road Junction U.17.a.45.90 - Road Junction U.11.b.2.3 (all inclusive to 2/7th)

7. (a) 2/4th will form up 100 yards in rear of 2/6th in Artillery formation.
B Coy. on RIGHT + D on LEFT will form 1st + 2nd waves
A " " " + C " " " " 3rd + 4th "

(b) Dividing line between Coys. will be line from U.21.c.15.25. - U.26.b.4.5. - U.21.b.0.3. - Trench Junction U.15.d.95.40 - Trench Junction U.16.c.10.45 - Junction Road and Trench U.16.c.3.6. (all above inclusive to D Coy.) - thence to houses at WESTERN extremity of the village U.11.c.2.2. (inclusive to C Coy.) thence to U.11.a.25.00.

'C' Coy. RIGHT platoon   HOUSES at WESTERN edge of
                         STREET about U.11.c.1.2.
'C' Coy. LEFT platoon   CEMETERY & BRICKWORKS in
                         U.10.d.

A & C Coys. will detail moppers up to deal with the STREET
these Coys. must continue to follow the barrage
It is the duty of B. Coy. to clear up and search the houses,
cellars and dugouts in the street.

8.   Touch must be maintained throughout whole advance
     with Units on RIGHT and LEFT flanks.

9. (a) Rate of advance is governed by barrage time table as shown
        on attached Map and is at rate of 2 minutes per 100 yards
    (b) The vital importance of keeping the closest possible on to
        the heels of barrage must be most strongly impressed on
        all ranks.
    (c) Officers and NCOs will move in line with, and not in
        front or rear, of their platoons.
    (d) OC. Coys. are reminded that on reaching line U.17.c.2.9.
        - U.10.c.7.0. - the barrage commences to swing forward
        on LEFT whilst remaining stationery on RIGHT
        This will necessitate RIGHT Coys. almost halting while
        LEFT Coys. get forward
        OC. Coys. must be most careful not to lose direction
        owing to this swinging barrage.

10. After capture of 3rd objective
    (a) A & C Coys. will select suitable positions to act as covering
        troops to B & D Coys. while latter are making Posts
    (b) B & D Coys. will construct Posts as under :-

Coy	Post No.	Position	Garrison
B	13	U.11.a.4.6.	1 Platoon
B	14	U.11.b.1.2.	" 1 M.G.
B	15	U.11.c.8.9.	"
B	16	U.11.c.4.6.	"
D	17	U.11.c.0.4.	"
D	18	U.10.d.7.7.	" 1 M.G.
D	19	U.16.b.9.7.	"
D	20	U.17.a.33	"

27

(c) At ZERO minus 8 minutes all Bns. of 186th will advance to line of road U.20.a.67.55 - U.20.d.9.4. where outer flanks will check slightly to allow centre to get up into general line of Roadway.
Barrage which opens at ZERO hour will regulate advance from this point

(d) At ZERO plus 1 hour and 15 minutes, 2/7th and 2/6th will have formed up EAST of 1st objective and will move forward in extended order keeping up close under barrage to line of 2nd objective.
The 1st and 2nd waves will be responsible for capture of 2nd objective
The 1st and 2nd waves (B & D Coys.) will advance to trench U.16.c. - U.15.d -
They will be responsible for mopping up this trench, posting sentries over dugouts, destroying tunnel (if any) and blocking flanks of trench. The moppers up will not enter the dugouts, nor leave their posts until relieved by 2/8th West Yorks.
The 3rd & 4th waves (A & C Coys.) will pass through 1st & 2nd waves and form up EAST of 2nd objective under barrage in readiness for subsequent advance on 3rd objective.
These two Coys. will then form 1st and 2nd Waves, B & D Coys. becoming 3rd and 4th waves.
Advance on 3rd objective will be commenced at ZERO plus 2 hours & 15 minutes - at which hour barrage will lift

(e) In attacking HENDECOURT the following are objectives for platoons of leading Coys.
A Coy. both RIGHT and LEFT platoons
  1st WOOD about U.17.a.1.7.
  2nd STREET and HOUSES U.17.a.45.90 - U.11.c.1.2.

under:-

 (a) Parade .... 9.30 pm
   Pass Coy. Point L'ABBAYE MORY .. 10.30 pm
   Reach Bde. Dump .... 12.50 am 12.30 am
   Clear   "   " .... ~~1.50 pm~~ thence
                        to forming up line

 (b) Order of march
   Hdqrs; B; D; C; carrying parties of C+D; A; carrying parties of A+B.

 (c) Route along North side and clear of MORY–ECOUST Road in B.17.b – B.12.c+d – C.1.c+d – to road immediately SOUTH of CEMETERY – crossing C.2.& 3.q. – thence to forming up tape.

 (d) Intervals of 50 yards to be maintained between Platoons – Touch to be kept by connecting files –

 (e) Men detailed to pick up stores from Bde. Dump to march on left, to facilitate picking up

 (f) No halts to be made EAST of MORY other than regulation halts at 10 minutes to the hour

 (g) Bn. will be marching in rear of 2/5th.

11. **Prisoners**   Escort at rate of 2 men for 10 prisoners. Prisoners will only be searched for arms. Officers will be searched for papers at once. All prisoners will be sent to Bde. Dump, and receipts obtained

12. **Police**   Sgt. Denby, Ptes. Kenyon, Knapton, Mundy, will be responsible for the collection and conducting to Divisional Stragglers Station any stragglers detained at Road junction at ERVILLERS at B.13.d.2.3. The Stragglers Station is at Behagnies H.2.a.5.q.

                       J. B. Ellison
                       Capt. +Adj
                       2/4

     from BD.
4 Guides/Reps ~~report~~ B.H.Q.
– 6.0 pm Z night to guide new W.P. to Posts.

Instructions

1. **Rations** — All ranks will carry unexpended portion of day's rations, the iron ration and a second iron ration. These iron rations are not to be consumed without C.O's orders.

2. **Hot Meal.** — O.C. Coys & HQ Coy. will see that a hot meal is issued as late as possible before leaving Camp.

3. **Water** — All bottles will be carried filled. A reserve of 500 tins will be available at L'ABBAYE MORY for issue to Bns. on evening after attack.

4. **Rum** — will be carried under Coy. arrangements and issued after Bn. has reached forming up tape.

5. **S.A.A. & Grenades** — The Bde. Dump is at O.2.d.1.8.

6. **Stores to be carried:**

   (a) Mills Grenades — Every man 2 bombs in breast pocket (Except Bn. Runners & Bn. Signallers). Bombers — 8 bombs in buckets.

   (b) Rifle Grenades — 8 per Rifle Grenadier in buckets.

   (c) Sandbags — 2 per man — rolled attached to braces.

   (d) Flares — 1 per man in left side pocket.

   (e) Wire Cutters } 10 per Company — selected men —
       Hedging gloves } fastened to belt.

   (f) Very pistols — One with each Officer and Platoon Commander of B & D Coys. — remainder with Officers of A & C Coys.

   Two men will be detailed to accompany each Officer or Platoon Commander, carrying 18 green lights each. O.C. B & D Coys. when consolidating will see that each Post has a Very pistol and sufficiency of white and green lights.

   (g) P. Bombs — One to be carried by each Officer and NCO.

   (h) Shovels } A & C Coys. 20 shovels — 10 picks } to be carried
       Picks }   B & D   .   30 shovels 10 picks } by rear waves of each Coy.

   (j) Platoon Flag — 1 per platoon.

   (k) Wire breakers — All available will be carried.

   (l) Field Dressing & Ampoule — By every Officer, NCO & man.

   (m) S.O.S. Signal — **GREEN** lights on rockets.

(n) Brigade Carrying Parties

	Strength	Duty	Report to	Hour
o	1 Officer	Carrying to	Capt. Bruce at	ZERO
+	2 N.C.Os	Advanced	Brigade Dump	"
+	25 O.R.	Battn.	C.2.z.1.8.	2 hours
*	2 Runners	Between Bde. & advanced Bn. Dumps	do	do

- o 2/Lt Lister
- + 1 N.C.O 13 men B Coy.
- + 1 N.C.O 12 men D Coy.
- * 1 man B Coy
- * 1 man D Coy

(o) Battalion Carrying parties

Mats 20 B Coy } Will be issued at Bde. Dump
      20 D Coy } C.2.z.1.8.

They will be carried by men of the leading waves as far as the 1st objective

Trench Bridge — 1 per Coy — will be issued at Bde. Dumps C.2.z.1.8.

(p) Coy. carrying parties

Party of 1 N.C.O and 10 men to carry

1 bundle of 5 picks . . . . . . 1 man
1 bundle of 5 shovels . . . . . 1 man
40 Bandoliers S.A.A. . . . . . 4 men
20 L.G. Magazines in 8 carriers . 4 men

These stores to be drawn from Bn. Mobilization Store.

7. **Code names** — When sending messages code names will not be used

8. **Papers etc.** — No secret map, tracing or document of any value of Military importance will be taken into action

9. **Dugouts** — All captured Dugouts will be systematically searched by special patrols. An Officer will be in charge and should be accompanied by a Medical Orderly

10. **Move.** — Bn. will move to forming up position on taped line on Y/Z night in accordance with march Table as

(c). Major LEAROYD will go forward with an officer of 57th Field Coy. R.E. and a proportion of sappers.
He will take command of the Posts thus established and will be responsible for general consolidation.

(d). A & C Coys. will be withdrawn when these Posts are capable of offering resistance — and will be concentrated about U.16.c. central.

11. Attack will be supported by M.G.° of 213th M.G. Coy and when final objective has been gained these guns will be located as under

    (a) Factory   U.22.b.1.7.   2 guns
    (b) Roadway   U.17.a.8.0.   1 gun
    (c) Road junction   U.17.b.3.6.   1 gun
    (d) As in para 10.b   2 guns.

12. Tanks will assist in operation. They will follow Infantry as closely as possible but Infantry will not wait for Tanks.

13. 15th Squadron R.F.C. will provide contact Aeroplanes to patrol during operations.
These Aeroplanes will demand information from Infantry by signals on Klaxon Horns or by dropping white lights. Infantry will light red flares, or if flares are exhausted wave their helmets, to shew whereabouts.

14. Runner Relay Posts will be established at following points

    (a) Road junction   U.27.b.2.9.   4 runners
    (b) Junction Trench & Road   U.21.d.4.6.   4 runners
    (c) Factory   U.22.b.0.7.   4 runners
    (d) Road junction   U.17.a.5.2.   4 runners

2/Lieut. CORDINGLEY will establish these posts as advance progresses. The Relay Posts will not be withdrawn until Battn. is relieved.

15 (a) Report centres will be established as follows:-
    Advanced Bde. Report Centre   B.6.d.4.5.

            Battn. Report Centre   U. 21. c. 8.0 (Rly. Embankment)
            Aid Post   U. 28. c. 8.0.   do

   (b)   As soon as 2nd objective has been gained LT. FLETCHER
         with telephone will move forward to U.21.a.8.5.
         On attainment of 3rd objective he will lay a line from above
         point to about Factory where he will select a site for Bn. H. Qrs.
         as near as possible to line of Relay Posts.

   (c)   When 2nd objective has been gained Bn. H. Qrs. will move
         forward to forward trench of 1st objective about U.21.d.4.6.
         When 3rd objective has been gained Bn. H. Qrs. will move
         forward to about Factory
         As soon as Posts in 3rd objective are reported to be
         progressing Bn. H. Qrs. will move to vicinity of WOOD
         about U.17.a.0.6.

16 (a)   All Coy. H.Q. established in any captured dugouts
         cellars etc. will have a sentry posted over them to direct
         orderlies bringing messages and to give alarm in
         case of counter attack.

   (b)   On establishment they will inform Bn. H.Q. of their
         whereabouts giving co-ordinates

   (c)   Coy. runners must be informed of position of Bn. H. Q.
         all Coy. H.Q. and all Posts.

17   On outer flanks of Coys. forming leading waves there will
         be an Officer and an NCO whose sole duty is to maintain
         direction
         They will be provided with compasses and will know
         bearings of the advance.

                                          J. B. Ellison.
                                          Capt & Adjt.
                                          ½th Bn.

Copy No 1   OC. A Coy   9   CO.
        2   " B   10   2ic
        3   " C   11   R.S.O.
        4   " D   12   Liaison Officer
        5   S.O.   13   War Diary
        6   L.O.   14 } Adjutant
        7   T.O.   15 }
        8   Q.M.

Confidential Vol 6

War diary

of

2/4th Bn. Duke of Wellington's Regiment

From 1st June 1917 to 30th June 1917

Volume No. 6.

Original

H₀.
6.T
2 sheets

WAR DIARY or INTELLIGENCE SUMMARY

2/4 Duke of Wellington's Rgt. Army Form C. 2118

(Erase heading not required.)

Place	Date	Hour	Summary of Events and Information	Remarks and references to Appendices
Achiet-le-Petit.	June 17.		B & C Coys. made up to the strength of 3 Officers & 115 O.R. each took over the 2nd line of Defence on the Sole frontage. Capt H.N. WALLER in command.	J.S.L.
	19th		B & C Coys were relieved in the 2nd line of Defence by the 187th Bde.	J.S.L.
	26th		The Bn moved to FAVREUIL.	J.S.L.
FAVREUIL NOREUIL	27th		The Bn moved into the Support Line of the Sole Front & were situated as follows. Bn HQ C.10.c.8.9. A Coy C.4.c.3.0. B Coy C.16.a.4.3. C Coy C.9.d.6.8. D Coy C.10.c.6.8. Ref: Sheet 57E NW. The transport remained at FAVREUIL.	J.S.L.

H.S. Nelly Lt Col
Comdg 2/4 DoW Regt

1.7.17

7.T.
2 sheets

Vol 7

SECRET.

War diary

of

4th Bn. Duke of Wellingtons Regt.

from 1st July 1917   to   31st July 1917

Volume 7

WAR DIARY or INTELLIGENCE SUMMARY

2/4 Duke of Wellington's Regt. Army Form C. 2118.

Place	Date	Hour	Summary of Events and Information	Remarks and references to Appendices
In the Field	July 1st		The Bn. relieved the 2/5 D of Ws. Regt. in the left sub-sector of the left sector.	J.S.E.
"	3rd		Capt. H.N. WALLER was killed whilst reconnoitring his line.	J.S.E.
"	5th		The Bn. was relieved by the 2/5 G.L. Regt. & proceeded into Camp at FAVREUIL. Lt. H. WHARTON died from Pernicious Anaemia at the Base, Rouen.	J.S.E.
VAULX	13th		The Bn. moved to VAULX into billets in reserve to the Bde. in the J.S.E. Line.	
VAULX	21st		The Bn. moved into the Right Sub-Sector of the Right Sector, relieving the 2/5 D of Ws. Regt. B & C Coys in the front line, A & D Coys in support.	J.S.E.
In the Line	25th		Inter-Company relief. B & C Coys going into support & A & D Coys occupying the front line.	J.S.E.
"	27th		Major R.G. BUCHANAN left the Bn. to take up the duties of Commandant 186th Inf. Bde School, BEUGNATRE.	J.S.E.
"	29		The Bn. was relieved in the line by the 2/5 G.L. Regt. & proceeded into Camp at FAVREUIL.	J.S.E.
FAVREUIL	30th			

1.8.17

J.G. Micklethwait
Lt. Col.
Comdg 2/4 D of Ws. Regt.

Original.   Secret.   Vol 8

War Diary.
of
3/4th Bn. Duke of Wellington's Regiment

from 1st August 1917 to 31st August 1917.

Volume No 8

P.S. Whom appears to
in Lieut-Col.?
Cmdg 3/4 Bn. Duke of Wellington's Regt

WAR DIARY
or
INTELLIGENCE SUMMARY.

(Erase heading not required.)

1/4 Duke of Wellington Regt.   Army Form C. 2118.

Place	Date	Hour	Summary of Events and Information	Remarks and references to Appendices
FAVREUIL	Aug 3rd		Bn. moved into Support at Vraucourt, two Coys. in JOINT TRENCH, C10.A.3.4. approx. HdQrs. & one Coy. at VRAUCOURT, relieving the 2/6 West York Regt. One Coy. at Square Corner C10.c.65.90.	J.S.I.
VRAUCOURT	8th		The Bn. move into the Left Sub-sector of the Right sector, Bn. H.Q. at C.5.a.25.40, relieving the 2/5 Duke of Wellington Regt.	J.S.I.
In the Field	12th		The Bn. was relieved in the line by the 2/5 K.O.Y.L.I., & moved into D Camp FAVREUIL.	J.S.I.
FAVREUIL	20th		The Bn. moved into support of the Right (Bellecourt) Sub-sector of the Left sector. Two Coys. in Railway Reserve, two Coys. on the Ervust-Noreuil Rd. Bn. HdQrs. at Scout Church.	J.S.I.
"	20th		The following Officers reported for duty. 2/Lt. & H.A. Lodewe, 2/Lt. S. Bennett, 2/Lt. G.V. Peel, 2/Lt. P. Allanpp, 2/Lt. A. Ratcliffe, 2/Lt. L. Jones.	J.S.I.
In the Field	28th		The Bn. moved into the line in the right Sub-sector of the Left Sub-sector of the Left sector, 3 Coys. in the front line & one Coy. in Horse Shoe Reserve.	J.S.I.

H.D. Hartforth
26 Lt
Comdg 1/4 Bn D. of W. Regt.

SECRET.

WAR DIARY of

2/4th BN. DUKE OF WELLINGTON'S REGT.

From 1st September to 30th September 1917.

VOLUME 9

[signature]
Capt for Lt-Col.
Cmdg. 2/4th Bn. Duke of Wellington's Regt.

Army Form C. 2118.

2/4 Duke of Wellington's Regt.

WAR DIARY
or
INTELLIGENCE SUMMARY.
(Erase heading not required.)

Instructions regarding War Diaries and Intelligence Summaries are contained in F.S. Regs., Part II and the Staff Manual respectively. Title pages will be prepared in manuscript.

Hour, Date, Place	Summary of Events and Information	Remarks and references to Appendices
In the Field Sept 6th	The Bn was relieved in the Right out. Section of the Left Section (BULLECOURT) by the 2/5 Y & L, & moved into huts at FAVREUIL, No 6 Camp.	A.S.E.
FAVREUIL. Sept 13th	The Bn moved into Support of the Right out Sector, B. Coy to Right Sector, A Coy on Rly Embankment in C S A, B5, the Right Sector, A Coy on Rly Embankment at C.S.A. C&D Coys in Dewdrop on Rly Embankment. Bn H.Q.3 at Hobart Corner. Trench C10A & C11A & C11C. (Ref Sheet # 1/10000.)	A.S.E
In the Field. Sept 22.	Bn relieved the 2/5 D of 6 Regt in the line. A Coy in Sheffield Trench & Sheffield Support, B Coy from C.5 & 2.10.50 to C.5 & 8.6. C Coy in Halifax Support from C.11 & 2.5.25 to C.11 & 2.6. D Coy from C.S.A 6.6 to C.11 & 2.6, in Halifax Support. Bn H.Q.3 on Rly Embankment C.S A 33.	A.S.E
In the Field Sept 29th	The Bn here relieved in the line by the 2/4 Y & L & went into camp at FAVREUIL, No 6 Camp.	A.S.E.

[Signature]
Capt for Lt Col Comdg 2/4 D of W Regt.

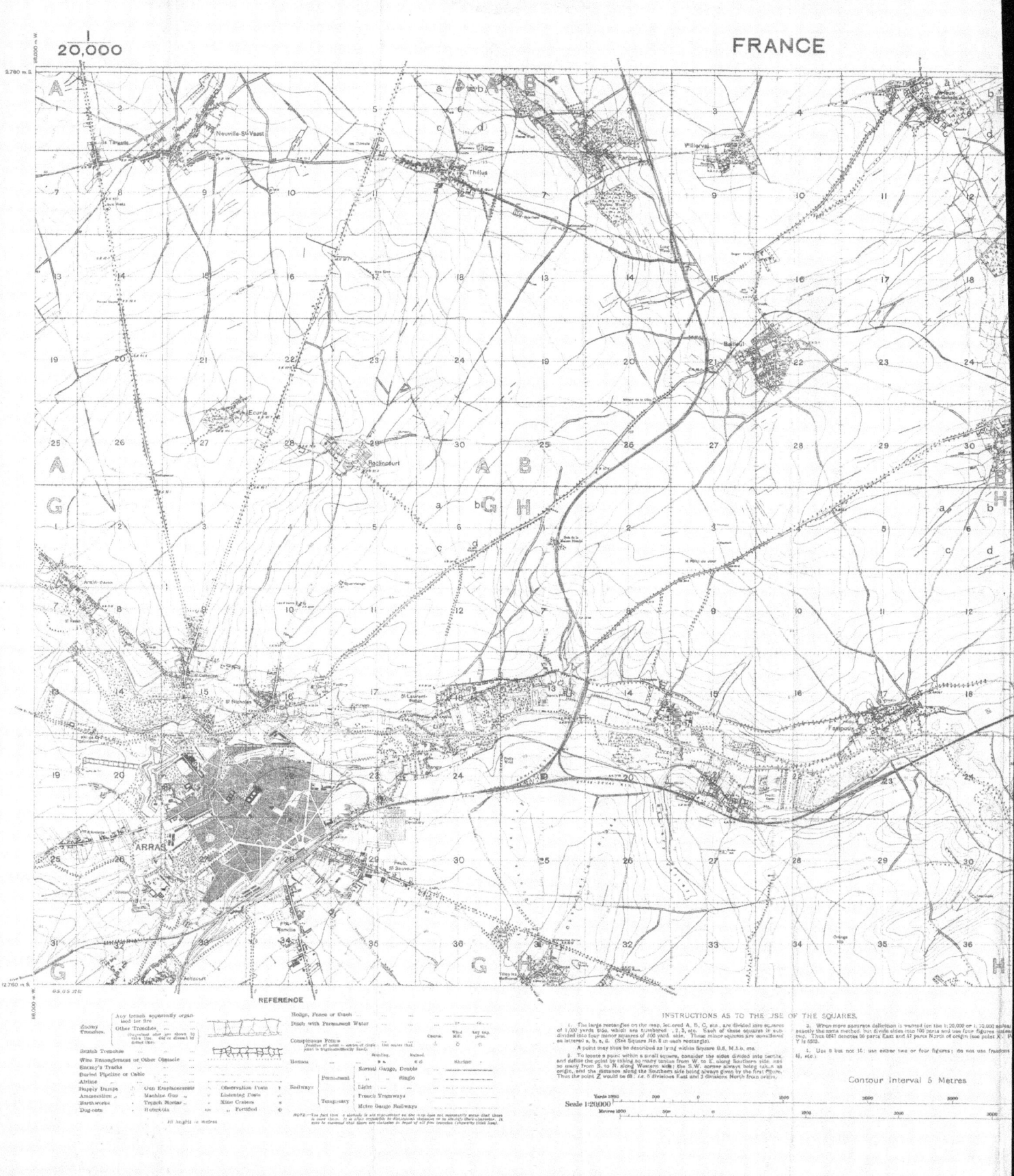

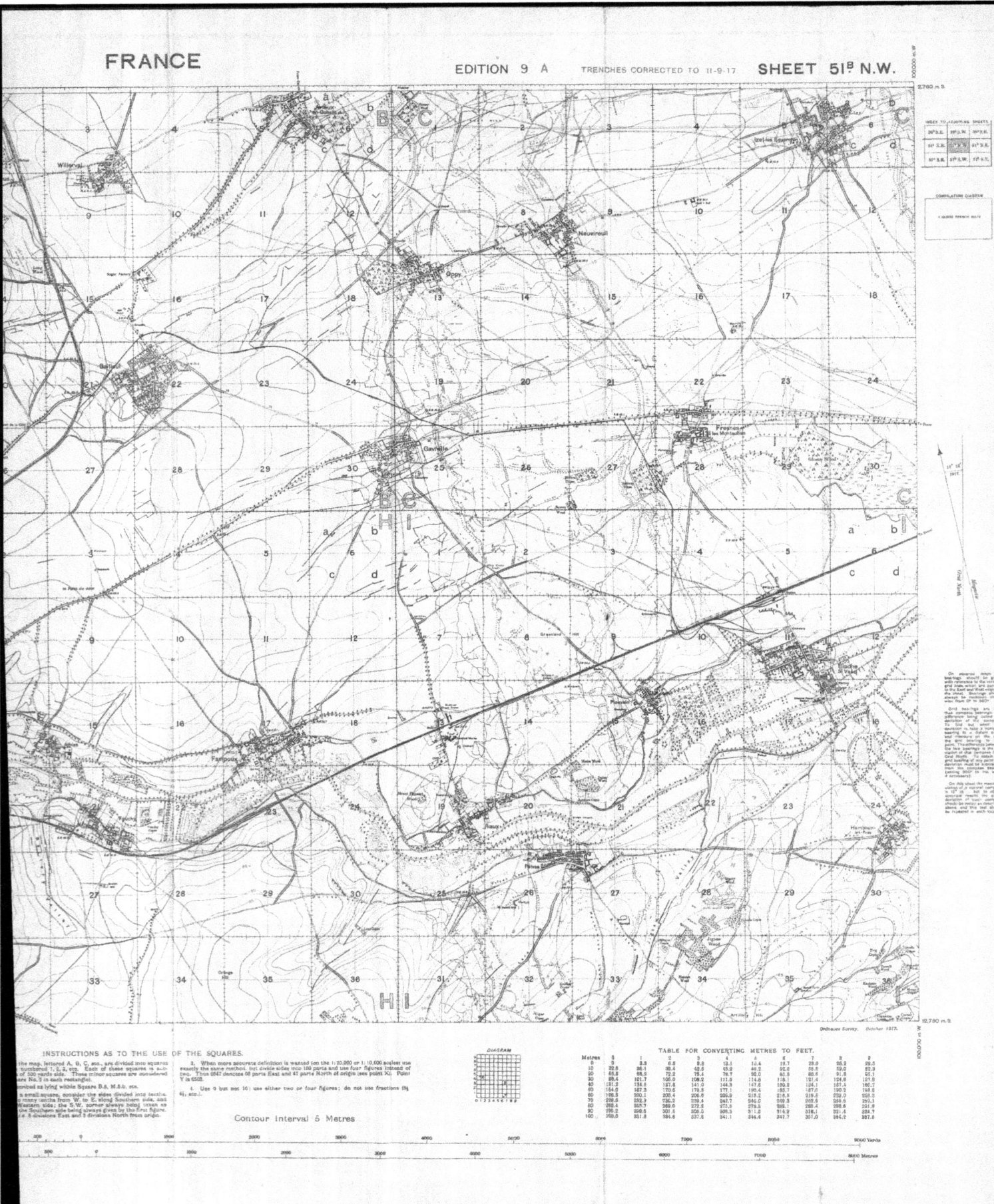

GLOSSARY.

Abbaye, Abb⁰	Abbey
Abreuvoir, Abʳ	Watering-place
Abri de douaniers	Custom-shelter
Aciérie	Steel works
Aiguilles	Points (Ry.)
Allée	Alley, Narrow road
Ancien - ne, Ancⁿ	Old
Aqueduc	Aqueduct
Arbre	Tree
— éventail	fan-shaped
— décharné	bare
— fourchu	forked
— isolé	isolated
— penché	leaning
Arbrisseau	Small tree
Arc	Arch
Ardoisière, Ardʳ	Slate quarry
Arrêt	Halt
Asile	Asylum
— des aliénés	Lunatic asylum
— de charité	
— des pauvres	Asylum
— de refuge	
Auberge, Aubᵉ	Inn
Aune	Alder-tree
Bac	Ferry
— à treille	
Bains	Baths
Place aux bains	Bathing place
Balise	Beacon
Banc de sable	Sand-bank
— vase	Mud-bank
Baraque	Hut
Barrage	Dam
Barrière	Gate, Rails
(Machine à) Bascule	Weigh-bridge
Bassin	Dock, Pond
— d'éclusage	Tidal dock
Bassin de radoub	Dry dock
Bateau phare	Light-ship
Blanchisserie	Laundry
B.M. (borne milliaire)	Mile stone
Bⁿ (borne kilométrique)	
Boulonnerie	Bolt Factory
Fabʳ de boulons	
Bouée	Buoy
Brasserie, Brassᵉ	Brewery
Briqueterie, Briqᵗ	Brickfield
Brise-lames	Breakwater
Bureau de poste	Post office
— de douane	Custom house
Butte	Butt, Mound
Cabane	Hut
Cabaret, Cabᵗ	Inn
Câble sous-marin	Submarine cable
Calvaire, Calvᵉ	Calvary
Canal de dessèchement	Drainage canal
Canal d'irrigation	Irrigation canal
Fabʳ de caoutchouc	Rubber factory
Carrière, Carʳ	Quarry
— de gravier	Gravel-pit
Caserne	Barracks
Champ de courses	Race-course
— manœuvres	Drill-ground
— tir	Rifle range
Chantier	Building yard
(Yard)	
Chantier de construction	Ship-way
Chapelle, Chᵉ	Chapel
Charbonnage	Colliery
Château d'eau	Water tower
Chaussée	Causeway, Highway
Chemin de fer	Railway
Cheminée, Chᵉᵉ	Chimney
Chêne	Oak tree
Cimetière, Cimᵉ	Cemetery
Clocher	Belfry
Clouterie	Nail factory
Colombier	Dove-cot
Cœur	
Cour des marchandises	Workmen's dwellings
— aux	Goods yard
Couvent	Convent
Crassier	Slag heap
Croix	Cross
Dame	Inner dock
Démoli - e	Destroyed
Détruit - e, Détᵗ	
Déversoir	Weir
Digue	Dyke, causeway
Distillerie, Distⁱᵉ	Distillery
Douane	Custom-house
Bureau de douane	Custom-house
Entrepôt de douane	Custom warehouse
Dynamitière, Dynamᵗ	Dynamite magazine
Dynamiterie	Dynamite factory
Écluse	Sluice, Lock
Écluses, Eclˢᵉˢ	Sluice
École	School
Écurie	Stable
Église	Church
Émaillerie	Enamel works
Embarcadère, Embʳ	Landing-place
Estaminet, Estamᵗ	Inn
Étang	Pond
Fabrique, Fabʳ	Factory
Fabʳ de produits chimiques	Chemical works
Fabʳ de faïence	Pottery
Faïencerie	Pottery
Ferme, Fᵐᵉ	Farm
Filature, Filᵉ	Spinning
Fonderie, Fondⁱᵉ	Foundry
Fontaine, Fontⁱᵉ	Spring, fountain
Forêt	Forest
Forme de radoub	Dry dock
Forge	Smithy
Fosse	Mine, Pit
Fossé	Moat, Ditch
Four	Kiln
— à chaux	Lime-kiln
Four à coke	Coke oven
Ganterie	Glove Factory
Gare	Station
Garenne	Warren
Garnison	Garrison
Gazomètre	Gasometer
Glacerie	Mirror Factory
Fabʳ de glaces	
Glacière	Ice factory
Grue	Crane
Gué	Ford
Guérite	Sentry-box, Turret
— à signaux	Signal-box (Ry.)
Halte	Halt
Hangar	Shed, Hangar
Hôpital	Hospital
Hôtel-de-Ville	Town hall
Houillère	Colliery
Huilerie	Oil factory
Imprimerie, Imprⁱᵉ	Printing works
Jetée	Pier
Laminerie	Rolling mills
Ligne de haute	Highwater mark
Laisse de basse marée	Low
Maison Forestière, Mᵒⁿ Fᵉᵉ	Forester's house
Maltrie	Malthouse
Marbrerie	Marble works
Marais	Marsh
Marais salant	Saltern, Salt marsh
Marché	Market
Mare	Pool
Meule	Rick
Minière	Mine
Monastère	Monastery
Moulin, Mⁿ	Mill
— à vapeur	Steam mill
Mur	Wall
— crénelé	Loop-holed wall
Navette	Ferry
Orme	Elm
Orphelinat	Orphanage
Ossuaire	Ossier-beds
Ouvrage	Fort
Ouvrages hydrauliques	Water works
Papeterie	Paper-mill
Parc	Park, yard
— aéronautique	Aviation ground
— à charbon	Coal yard
— à pétrole	Petrol store
Passage à niveau, P.N.	Level-crossing
Passerelle, Passʳᵉ	Foot-bridge
Pépinière	Nursery garden
Peuplier	Poplar tree
Phare	Light-house
Pilier, Pilʳ	Pier
Plaine d'exercices	Drill ground
Pompe	Pump
Ponceau	Culvert
Pont	Bridge
— levis	Drawbridge
Poste de garde	Guard
Station côtière	station
Poterie	Pottery
Poudrière, Poudʳᵉ	Powder magazine
Magasin à poudre	
Prise d'eau	Water supply
Puits	Pithead, Shaft, Well
— artésien	Artesian well
— d'airage	Ventilating shaft
— ventilateur	
— de sondage	Boring
Quai	Quay, Platform
— aux bestiaux	Cattle platform
— aux marchandises	Goods platform
Raccordement	Junction
Raffinerie	Refinery
— de sucre	Sugar refinery
Râperie	Beet-root factory

Four à coke	Coke oven.
Ganterie	Glove Factory.
Gare	Station.
Garenne	Warren.
Garnison	Garrison.
Gazomètre	Gasometer.
Glacerie	Mirror Factory.
Fabque de glaces	Ice factory.
Glacière	
Grue	Crane.
Gué	Ford.
Guérite	Sentry-box, Turret.
à signaux	Signal-box (Ry.)
Halle	Hall.
Hangar	Shed, Hangar.
Hôpital	Hospital.
Hôtel-de-Ville	Town-hall.
Houillère	Colliery.
Huilerie	Oil factory.
Imprimerie, Imprie	Printing works.
Jetée	Pier.
Laminerie	Rolling mills.
Ligne de haute...	
Laisse de haute marée	High water mark.
de basse marée	Low ...
Maison Forestière, Mon Fre	Forester's house.
Malterie	Malt-house.
Marbrerie	Marble works.
Marais	Marsh.
Marais salant	Saltern, Salt marsh.
Marché	Market.
Mare	Pool.
Meule	Rick.
Minière	Mine.
Monastère	Monastery.
Moulin, Mn	Mill.
à vapeur	Steam mill.
Mur	Wall.
crénelé	Loop-holed wall.

Nacelle	Ferry.
Orme	Elm.
Orphelinat	Orphanage.
Oseraies	Osier-beds.
Ouvrage	Fort.
Ouvrages hydrauliques	Water works.
Papeterie	Paper-mill.
Parc	Park, yard.
.. aérostatique	Aviation ground.
.. à charbon	Coal yard.
.. à pétrole	Petrol store
Passage à niveau P.N.	Level-crossing.
Passerelle, Pose	Foot-bridge.
Pépinière	Nursery-garden.
Peuplier	Poplar tree.
Phare	Light-house.
Pilier, Pilr	Post.
Plaine d'exercice	Drill ground.
Pompe	Pump.
Ponceau	Culvert.
Pont	Bridge.
.. levis	Drawbridge.
Poste de garde	
Station côte	Coast-guard station.
Poteau Pu	Post.
Poterie	Pottery.
Poudrière, Poudre	Powder magazine.
Magasin à poudre	
Prise d'eau	Water supply.
Puits	Pit-head, Shaft, Well.
.. artésien	Artesian well.
.. d'airage	
.. ventilateur	Ventilating shaft.
.. de sondage	Boring.
Quai	Quay, Platform.
.. aux bestiaux	Cattle platform.
.. aux marchandises	Goods platform.
Raccordement	Junction.
Raffinerie	Refinery.
.. de sucre	Sugar refinery
Raperie	Beet-root factory.

Remblai	Embankment.
Remise des Machines	Engine-shed.
Réservoir, Rr	Reservoir.
Route cavalière	Bridle road.
Rubanerie	Ribbon Factory.
Ruines	
En ruine	Ruin.
Ruiné	
Sablière	Sand-pit.
Sablonnière, Sablonre	
Sapin	Fir tree.
Saule	Willow tree.
Saunerie	Salt-works.
Scierie, Scie	Saw-mill.
Sondage	Boring.
Source	Spring.
Sucrerie, Sucre	Sugar factory
Tannerie	Tannery.
Tir à la cible	Rifle range.
Tissage	Weaving mill
Tôlerie	Rolling mill
Tombeau	Tomb.
Tour	Tower.
Tourbière	Peat-bog, Peat-bed.
Tourelle	Small tower.
Tuilerie	Tile works.
Usine à gaz	Gas works.
.. électrique d'électricité	Electricity works.
.. métallurgique	Metal works.
.. à agglomérés	Briquette factory.
Verrerie, Verre	Glass works.
Viaduc	Viaduct.
Vivier	Fish Pond.
Voie de chargement	
.. déchargement	
.. d'évitement	Siding.
.. formation	
.. manœuvre	
Zinguerie	Zinc works.

TRENCH MAP.

FRANCE.

SHEET 51ᴮ N.W.

EDITION 9. A

INDEX TO ADJOINING SHEETS

SCALE 1/20,000.

Confidential.

War Diary
of
2/4th Bn Duke of Wellington's Regt.

From:- 1st October 1917   To:- 31st October 1917.

(Volume 10)

J.W. Walsh Lieut-Colonel
Commanding 2/4th Bn Duke of Wellington's Regt.

Army Form C. 2118.

WAR DIARY
or
INTELLIGENCE SUMMARY.
(Erase heading not required.)

2/4 Duke of Wellington's Regt.

Place	Date	Hour	Summary of Events and Information	Remarks and references to Appendices
FAVREUIL	Oct 7		The Bn. relieved the 2/4 KOYLI in the Centre Sector of the Divl: Sector (BULLECOURT).	J.S.L.
In the field	10th		The Bn. was relieved in the line by the 28th:Ship Inginf. and went into he 6 Camp FAVREUIL.	J.S.L.
In the field	12th		The Bn. moved into "A" Camp BEAULENCOURT.	J.S.L.
BEAULENCOURT	30th		The Bn. moved to GOMIECOURT, Carlton Hill Camp.	J.S.L.
GOMIECOURT	31st		The Bn. moved to SIMENCOURT, into 'A' Camp.	J.S.L.
SIMENCOURT	31st		Major E.C. Learoyd was appointed second in command of the Battn. from Oct 5/19.	J.S.L.

A.E.Shord Lt Col
C.C. 2/4 Duke of Wellington's Regt

SECRET

2/L W Reading ?

Wednesday 11 & 1915

Nov 11 1915

11.T.
26 shots

On His Majesty's Service.

SECRET

D.A.G. BASE

Original   Vol 11

War Diary

— of —

2/4th Bn. Duke of Wellington's (W.R.) Reg.t (T.F.)

From 1st November 1917 to 30th November 1917

Volume 12.

H.S. Mon[...]
Lieut Col
2/4 Duke of Wellington's

Army Form C. 2118.

1/4 Duke of Wellington's Regt.

WAR DIARY
or
INTELLIGENCE SUMMARY.
(Erase heading not required.)

Instructions regarding War Diaries and Intelligence Summaries are contained in F. S. Regs., Part II. and the Staff Manual respectively. Title pages will be prepared in manuscript.

Place	Date	Hour	Summary of Events and Information	Remarks and references to Appendices
	Nov.			
SIMENCOURT	14/17		The Battⁿ moved from SIMENCOURT to ACHIET-LE-PETIT, marching by night.	J.A.E.
ACHIET-LE-PETIT	16		The Battⁿ moved from ACHIET-LE-PETIT marching by night to LECHELLE.	J.A.E.
LECHELLE	18th		The Battⁿ moved from LECHELLE to BERTINCOURT marching by night. The 62nd Div. having taken ground to attack HAVRINCOURT & the vicinity of HAVRINCOURT WOOD. The Batⁿ moved up to HAVRINCOURT WOOD and after a short halt	J.S.E.
BERTINCOURT	20th		advanced to their objectives, namely the village of GRAINCOURT & the FACTORY E29a.5.8 (Ref: MOEUVRES Special Sheet 1:20000) which were taken by Companies as follows. GRAINCOURT by C & D Coys. under Lt. J.H. Sims & 2/Lt. P.A. Brown respectively. The FACTORY by B Coy under Lt to Knowles. The enemy making a determined resistance. During the operation about 130 prisoners were taken & eleven guns made up as follows 2 8" How^{rs}; 2 5.9" How^{rs}. 7 Field guns, also 13 Machine Guns. Our casualties amounted to 1 Officer killed, 2 wounded, 2 50 other ranks killed & wounded. Posts were established NORTH & NORTH EAST of the FACTORY & also on the NORTH, NORTH EAST & NORTH WEST of GRAINCOURT. A Coy under Lt. N. L. Oldroyd were kept in reserve at K.5.a.5.4. (Ref. MOEUVRES Sheet 1:20000)	J.S.E.

WAR DIARY
or
INTELLIGENCE SUMMARY

Army Form C. 2118.

2/4 Duke of Wellington Regt

Place	Date	Hour	Summary of Events and Information	Remarks and references to Appendices
(Ref. MOEUVRES Sheet 1 – 20000)	21st		At 10.30 A.m. on the morning of the 21st inst the Batt'n advanced to take the village of ANNEUX & the line of trenches from J.20.c.1.3 to road at E.24.b.8.6. C & A Coys operating on the right flank including the village of ANNEUX & B & D Coys operating on the left flank. Four tanks preceded C & A Coys into the village which was strongly held by machine guns & which was stubbornly defended. C & A Coys cleared the village by about 1pm but having had considerable casualties & finding the enemy in considerable force could make no further progress & so consolidated North & North East of the village. B & D Coys also met considerable resistance at the NORTH WEST of the village, & suffered many heavy casualties, but finally reached their objective, namely the enemy trench from E.24.b.8.6. to F.19.a.9.5. (approx) which proved to be a dummy trench. This necessitated B & D Coys withdrawing to the Sunken Rd about E.24.d.8.5. to E.24.c.10.20. The Batt'n has relieved about 8pm by the 2/7 West Yorks. About 200 prisoners were captured during the day & a number of machine guns destroyed. Our casualties were about 6 officers wounded & 120 other ranks killed & wounded.	J.R.L.

WAR DIARY
or
INTELLIGENCE SUMMARY.
(Erase heading not required.)

Army Form C. 2118.

1/4 Batt/ of Seaforth Highlanders

Hour, Date, Place	Summary of Events and Information	Remarks and references to Appendices
GRAINCOURT. Nov 21st Continued.	(Ref. MOEUVRES Sheet 1 - 20000) Batt. after being relieved moved to about K5 a 5.3 where the Batt. "dug-in".	J.M.L.
Nov 22nd	The Bt moved into trenches in HAVRINCOURT WOOD.	J.M.L.
Nov 23rd	The Bt moved into billets in BERTINCOURT.	J.M.L.
Nov 25-26.	The Bt moved into support of the line South of BOURLON WOOD. A Coy being in cellars in ANNEUX, B Coy in the SUNKEN ROAD E24b 2.6 to E24 b 10.20, C & D Coys in the SUNKEN ROAD E24 b 11.3 to E24 d 9.0.	
Nov 27th	The 62nd Divi were ordered to continue the attack in conjunction with the Divisions on their flanks. The 186th Bde area was BOURLON WOOD. The advance was only a partial success. The Bt were held in readiness throughout the day, in support, to deal with enemy counter-attacks, in F.13.b, & suffered heavily from the enemy barrage, having 6 Officers wounded & 170 other ranks killed wounded & missing.	J.M.L.

WAR DIARY or **INTELLIGENCE SUMMARY.** Army Form C. 2118.

7th Duke of Wellington's Rgt.

Hour, Date, Place	Summary of Events and Information	Remarks and references to Appendices
In the Field, Nov 28th	(Ref MOEUVRES Sht. 1-20000.) The Bt. moved into reserve at K.9 & 3.2.	J.S.S.
Dec 2nd	The Bn. moved into a trench running from K.8.a.7.6 to K.8.6.8.8 approx. (not shown on maps) & contracted posts.	J.S.S.
		H.E.P.Nash. Lt. Col. Comdg. 7/4 Duke of Wellington's Rgt.
	A detailed narrative of the operations is attached as an appendix.	7/4 Duke of Wellington's Rgt.

2/6th Bn.

TABLE "A"

ORDERS TO BE NOTED

1. Dress and Equipment — 62nd Divl. Battle Standing Orders paras. 1 & 3.

2. Officers' dress. — S.S.135 para XXI (i) (Clothing optional)

3. Prisoners. — S.S.135 para. XXVI (Size of escort amended to 5%)

4. Wounded. — S.S.135 para. XXVII. No unwounded man, other than Stretcher bearers, is allowed to bring back wounded men. Unwounded men, who are not Stretcher Bearers, and who are found bringing back wounded men will be treated as Stragglers.

5. Enemy Ruses — S.S.135 para XXVIII.

    White flag. Should the enemy put up the White flag, no notice should be taken of it until they actually come out unarmed and with their hands up, when they will be passed through our lines as prisoners.

    Holding on. The word "Retire" does not exist, and will not be understood or obeyed by anyone in this Division. The use of this word by the enemy has caused us disaster in the past or led to great confusion and loss. When once the advance has begun all ranks should be imbued with the spirit of going on to their objective. It is far harder, as a rule, to hold on to a captured position than it is to capture it, but it invariably costs more to retire than it does to hold on. If it is possible to retire, it is generally possible to reinforce and hang on.
    To retire means to abandon our wounded.
    An hostile counterattack is the finest test of our discipline.
    It will never succeed in the face of well directed rapid rifle fire.
    It is fatal to retire in the face of machine gun fire.
    As a rule fewer casualties are suffered by rushing an enemy machine gun than by lying down.

6. Distinguishing Marks — S.S.135 para XXXII. (There will be no moppers up)

7. Documents & maps. — S.S.135 para. XXXII. No documents or letters, official or _private_, should be carried on the person when going into action. The only maps to be carried will be notified by Div. H.Q.

8. Signalling to Aeroplanes. — S.S.135. Appx. "B" Reference Table 1 (1). The colour of light which will be used will be notified separately.

9. Trophies. 62nd Divl. Battle Standing Orders. Sec.6.
Trophy hunting by the troops after reaching their objective must be stopped. It causes men to get out of hand instead of consolidating and preparing to meet a hostile counter-attack. It has been the cause of losing a hard-won position.

Captured Machine Guns. If in working order, should be handed over with their ammunition as soon as possible to the nearest Brigade Machine Gun team, so that they may be used against the enemy.

10. Water. 62nd Divl.Battle Standing Orders. Sec.11. Men should be made to exercise restraint in drinking from their Water Bottles.

11. Flanks. The protection of the flanks of each Unit or formation,however small,is of vital importance.
Each Unit should protect its own flanks and not leave them unguarded because troops of other Units are supposed to be on either flank. This applies specially to the outer flanks of Units on the flanks of a Brigade.
Special arrangements should be made by each Unit to protect its flanks in case they are at any time "in the air". An exposed flank does not justify retirement. It can usually be made secure by a block or strong point with a Lewis Gun.
It is important to keep touch on the flanks and to keep direction. Personnel should be detailed specially on each flank for the purpose of keeping direction.

12. Information. Sending back information as often as possible in the attack. Negative information often of great value.
No information is likely to lead to no assistance - therefore,when in a tight place,send back information.
Information of special importance should always be sent in duplicate by different routes,or by different methods e.g., by runner - each runner proceeding by a different route - or by runner and carrier pigeon.
The correct writing of messages and reports should be practised till it becomes habitual.
The sender must state the time of despatch and his position at time of writing,otherwise message is likely to be of little value.

13. Patrols. S.S.172,para.9 (b) ("Preliminary Notes on Recent operations on front of Second Army")
It is a principle which should never be ignored that patrols are pushed out after the gaining of the final objective.
Even if it is impossible for them to pass through the stationary "protective" barrage at once,they should always be able to do so as soon as this has slackened down to fire on selected points. These patrols cover the work of consolidation,keep touch with the enemy,look out for making further small gains to improve our position, and give early warning of a counter attack.

14. Mutual support. Platoon and Section Commanders should be on the look out for opportunities of providing mutual support to each other in the attack,e.g.,
(a) If one part of the line is held up by Machine Gun Fire,it may be possible for another part of the line to push forward,and engage the hostile machine gun from a flank.

(b) Section Columns, defiling through gaps in the enemy wire made by the Tanks, should be covered by Lewis Gun Sections on the flanks of the gap.

NOTE. The foregoing are only a few of the more important points. Officers must have a thorough grasp of all the various instructions contained in S.S.135 which apply to them, also of the Divisional Battle Standing Orders.

[signature]

Capt. & Adjt.
2/4th Bn.

17.11.17.

2/4TH BATTALION

INSTRUCTIONS

1	Information	The general plan of operations has been explained to all concerned.
		The line is believed to be held very lightly. The boundary between the 84th R.I.R. and the 274th R.I.R. lately known as holding the line – is the road running from TRESCAULT through K.35.c & a to K.29.d
2	Personnel	(a) Personnel to be left out is separately detailed in Table "C"
		(b) Officers for Liaison
		186th Inf. Bde. Hd. Qrs. .... 2/Lt H Radcliffe
		Left Bn. 51st Divn. .... 2/Lt V L Patch
3	Surplus Kits	Packs will be clearly marked in indelible pencil shewing man's No. name Coy. and Bn. Blankets rolled in bundles of 10 will be securely tied and labelled
		Coy. and Bn. property will be clearly marked
		The whole of the above to be handed over to Q.M. Stores by midnight Y.Z. day
		1 N.C.O. and 3 men (2 per Coy) Table "C" will be left in charge of these stores at the Bn Dump in METZINCOURT. The Quartermaster will give them 2 days rations after which time they will be rationed by the Town Major.
4	Dress & Equipment	As laid down in 62nd Divl Battle Standing Orders with the following additions and amendments :-
		Entrenching tool in front
		Cardigan worn
		Jerkin rolled inside the waterproof sheet and attached to the waistbelt
		Box respirators and not P.H. Helmets will be taken into action.
		Each N.C.O. and man will carry an adequate supply of flannelette and oil
		Haversack Contents of :-
		Washing and shaving kit
		Iron rations
		Rations for 1 day (grocery ration in Mess tin
		1 Tommy Cooker
		Every N.C.O. and man 2 sandbags fastened under flap of haversack
		Bomb Buckets All Bombers and R. Grenadiers.
		All available Wire cutters and breakers will be carried – distribution by Coy Commanders.
		Very Pistols – two per Platoon.
		Compasses.
		Field Glasses.
		Baton. & Coy. Hd Qrs. one Lantern
		Tape Each Platoon Commander one roll of 50 yd
		All vigilant periscopes – distribution by Coy. Commanders.

The Quartermaster will arrange for the following Stores to be collected at the Battalion Transport Lines and held in readiness to be sent forward at short notice.

Barr & Stroud Range finders
Box periscopes
Telescopic Sighted rifles.
Supply of flannelette and oil.
Leading tape.
Supply of water in petrol tins sufficient for 24 hours consumption.

1. **Dumps.** **S.A.A. & Grenades.**
Divisional Dumps will be at P.9.d.9.1. and I.22.b.1.7
Brigade Dumps will be in HAVRINCOURT WOOD at Q.8.b
central and Q.1.c. central.

R.E.Stores.
Divisional Reserve Dump RUYAULCOURT, P.9.d.9.1.
Advanced Dumps HAVRINCOURT WOOD
    (a) B.w.26.   K.31.c.1.
    (b) Between B.w.60 & B.w.62 at Q.7.b.

51st Divl.Advanced Dump.
    (a) B.w.54.   A.10.a.
    (b) TRESCAULT

Corps Water Supply.
Left - NEUVMY
Right - METZ
Main - BERTINCOURT.

5. **Supplies.** Ration supply will be normal. Rations for Z. day will be drawn from Q.M. Stores on Y. day. They will be issued to each individual Officer, N.C.O. & man.

7. **Rations on Z day.** The Quartermaster will arrange for a hot breakfast meal to be provided about 3am on Z day so that each man shall advance with a complete day's ration on him. This breakfast meal will consist of Tea, sugar, Preserved Meat, Potted meat or Fish. The Quartermaster will arrange for a certain amount of bread to be taken from the rations of "X" & "Y" days for this extra meal.
Iron rations will on no account be touched without orders from Battalion Headquarters.

Rum. An issue of rum will be made on Y/Z night and will be issued with the breakfast meal on "Z" day.

8. **Police Traffic control stragglers & Prisoners of War**
Traffic control posts will be established at :-
1. I.1.c.9.2.
2. B.7.b.9.5.
3. P.7.b.0.4.
4. P.2.a.0.4.
5. P.10.a.9.5.
6. P.10.c.5.8.
7. P.15.b.3.4.
Stragglers Posts will be established at :-
1. J.34.d.9.5.
2. P.10.a.9.5.
3. P.17.A.0.5.
Stragglers collecting station will be at
P.10.c.5.9.
Prisoners of War pen (Corps) will be at
RUYAULCOURT
Divisional collecting station will be at :-
1. ~~~~~~~~~ Q.8.a.1.9. 100" N. of CLAYTON CROSS.
2. ~~Q.15.a.9.6~~
Coys. will send Prisoners of War direct to advanced Brigade Headquarters, which will be established in N.E. corner of HAVRINCOURT.
Receipts for prisoners will invariably be obtained and given when change of escort is carried out. Every use will be made of Prisoners of War for carrying any wounded. Prisoners will be disarmed before being sent to Brigade Headquarters (Advance) Officers will be searched for papers, documents &c.which will be forwarded with escort to Advanced Brigade Headquarters.
Other ranks will not be searched except for Arms Bombs,&c.

Escort for conducting prisoners from Advanced
Brigade Headquarters to Divisional Collecting
stations will consist of the following :-
    Sgt. Denby.   "B" Coy.
    Cpl. Whitaker) "A" Coy.
    10 men   )
This party will report at Brigade Headquarters at
Zero plus 2 hours and all ranks must know the
location of the two Divisional collecting stations.

11. **Casualties.** Reports will be sent in two forms as under :-
    1. Estimated casualty return
         Each casualty report will include total
         estimated casualties from Zero hour.
         Numbers missing who are believed to be
         prisoners to be stated in each report.
    2. Daily casualty return.
         Due at Battalion H.Q. at 8pm, detailing
         actual casualties determined.

The reporting of estimated casualties by Coys
to Bn.Hd.Qrs. is of special importance, and on this
depends the supply of reinforcements.
The estimate should be made at the earliest
possible moment after heavy casualties occur and
reported as soon as possible to Bn.HdQrs. Room
nos. are to be given, Officers and other ranks
separately. No distinction is to be made between
killed, wounded and missing.

12. **Rations routes & supply.** As soon as the situation permits on "Z" day the
Transport Officer will reconnoitre all routes up
to the present front line.
On the evening of Z day and each succeeding day
the procedure for delivery of supplies will be
as follows :- Brigade Headquarters will arrange
a rendezvous for all Transport and Bn.Hd.Qrs.
and the Transport Officer will be informed of the
location and time of this rendezvous.

13. **Collection & disposal of dead.** This will be arranged by the Divisional Burials
Officer. The Divisional Cemetery will be at about
J.26.a.b.2. 1 N.C.O. and 9 men will be required
for burial work - See Table "D".

14. **Salvage & Reinforcements** The Second in Command will arrange for a
party from details left behind, to reconnoitre
as early as possible the forward area for valuable
articles such as are likely to be urgently required
by the Battalion in refitting. He will also
hold in readiness two guides available to proceed
to ROCQUIGNY, when required, to conduct reinforcements
from the Corps Reinforcement Camp. On arrival
guides will report at the Camp Commandant's Office.

15. **Ground flares & S.O.S. Signals.** The ground flare and S.O.S. Signal to be used
will be as follows :-
    Ground flares - White.
    S.O.S. Signal. 1" Corps Rifle Grenade
                 bursting into 2 Red & 2
                 White.

16.	German documents	Coys. will arrange for special men to be told off to search German Corpses and dugouts for documents. The German Identity disc is made to break in half, one half remaining attached to the strap, the other half will be broken off and sent in with the documents to Advanced Brigade Head quarters from where they will be sent to the Divisional Intelligence Officer at the Divisional collecting station.
17.	Maps.	Reference Table A No.7, the following Maps only may be carried into action :- (1) MORTAGNES 1/20,000. (2) VALENCIENNES, 1/100,000. (3) Special Trench Maps Nos. 82 & 83. (4) Divisional message maps. (5) Brigade Message sketch maps.
18.	Synchronisation of watches.	All Officers will synchronise the time twice on Y day.
19.	Pigeons.	Pigeons will be issued to "B" & "C" Coys. These will be in charge of the Coy. pigeoneer who will remain with the O.C. Coy. Birds are for use on Z day and any birds not used by 3pm Z day must be released. One bird should be released as soon as objective is reached. Messages must not be written in indelible pencil.

J. B. Ellison
Capt. & Adjt.
7/4th Bn.

TABLE "B"

SCALE of S.A.A. &c to be carried.

	1	2	3	4	5	6	7	8	9	10	11
	S.A.A.	"P" Bombs.	No. 23 R.G's	20 or 24 R.G's	27 R.G's smoke	Very lights & shades	Ground flares	Revolver Ammn.	S.O.S. Grenades	No.5 Grenade	Pick or shovel
Coy. Officers		4a				6b	1	12			
Lewis (Nos. 1 & 2	50						1	12			
Gunners) Remainder	50						1				1c
Bombers	50	7a	8				1			4	1c
Rifle Grenadiers	50		3	5	1		1				
Riflemen	170		5ea 20?				1			1cr 1-23	1d
Section) Lewis Gun	50	1					1				
Commanders) Bombing	50	1	1	1			1				
) Riflemen	170	1					1				
Battn. Headquarters.									9		
Company Headquarters									9		

b. 6 per Very Pistol, 2 Very Pistols per Platoon. The second Very Pistol will be carried by an N.C.O. detailed by the Platoon Commander.

d. Each man of Rifle Sections will carry a pick or shovel, in the proportion of one pick to two shovels.

a. Company Commander excluded : also may not be available.

c. Two shovels per section of Lewis Gunners and Bombers will be carried.

Narrative of Operations 21st November 1917.
Capture of Anneux Village and Anneux Chapel
Cross Roads.

Reference map MOEUVRES 1/20.000.

I. **General.**

About 5 a.m. orders were received at Battalion Hdqrs for the further advance of the Brigade.

II. **Objectives.**

The Battalion objectives were the village of ANNEUX, ANNEUX CHAPEL and Cross Roads at E.19.c.2.9. with final objective along what subsequently transpired to be merely a spit-locked trench from F.20.c.1.3 to E.24.b.8.6.
Six Tanks were allotted for the entry into ANNEUX and these were to subsequently move to the left along the Battalion objective. A 20 minutes artillery barrage was put down on the objective and then lifted 400 yards beyond.
The Divisional Machine Gun Coy. also put down a barrage about F.19.d. and F.20.c. as soon as the infantry and the Tanks moved on Anneux, from the road in R.6.b.

III. **Dispositions of Attack.**

The Commanding Officer met Company Commanders in GRAINCOURT about 7 a.m. and issued verbal orders for the advance which was timed to take place at 10 a.m. 'C' Coy. with 'A' Coy. in support echeloned to the right were ordered to capture ANNEUX VILLAGE with final objective F.20.c.1.3 to F.19.b.0.5. 'B' Coy. with 'D' Coy. in support were ordered to capture ANNEUX CHAPEL with final objective F.19.b.0.5 to E.24.b.8.6. Hdqrs were to be established at GRAINCOURT CEMETERY E.30.c. (central)

IV. **Tanks.**

It was arranged with the officer commanding the Tanks that two tanks would move on either flank of the village and that two would go through the main street, each pair having one platoon of the infantry of the leading company following. Owing to the difficulties in traversing GRAINCOURT village the attack did not commence till about 10.20 a.m.

V. **The advance on & capture of ANNEUX VILLAGE.**

Led by the six Tanks as above described, 'C' Coy. advanced

on a three-platoon frontage followed by A' Coy. echeloned on the outh or (right) flank which was entirely in the air.

The enemy were holding the trenches south of the village in considerable force and offered strong opposition with machine gun fire, but on the near approach of the infantry they in some cases speedily surrendered, in others fought till they were wiped out with the bayonet.

The machine gun fire along the trenches on the Eastern side of the village gave the Tanks plenty of work but followed closely by the infantry sections all opposition was overcome.

In the village a considerable amount of sniping was met with from windows but the using of the Lewis Gun fired from the hip overcame this opposition and the platoon pushed on to the further end of the village, mopping up en route. The platoon which moved on the Western flank experienced considerable and more costly opposition from machine guns fire about the Chapel Cross Roads and found great difficulty in moving at one time.

C' Coy however were finally able to push through and establish themselves on the northern edges of the village where they re-organised preparatory to the further intended advance on the final objective.

No further progress could however be made, owing to numerous enemy machine guns placed in well camouflaged positions. Numerous enemy posts existed in F.19.c. & d. on the reverse slopes of the spur running N.E. while machine guns enfiladed any further advance from the vicinity of the chapel.

The supporting company meanwhile had moved forward well outside the South east edge of the village acting on the exposed flank which was in the air. They, after considerable mopping up of enemy parties, reached the line of the road about F.25.b.0.4. They similarly found any further advance impossible. The two company commanders thereupon decided to entrench and formed a series of posts around the N. and N.E. edges of the village. 'A' Coy. from about F.25.b.0.4 to Cross Roads F.25.a.5.9 C' Coy. from F.25.b.5.9. to F.25.a.1.7.

Both companies were subjected to heavy gun fire during the afternoon but escaped any direct hits on their posts.

VI Vickers Guns.

During the day 5 Vickers guns were sent up to assist in holding the village. 4 were placed on the Eastern flank about F.25 central while one gun came into action about F.25.a.3.8.

VII Advance on and capture of ANNEUX CHAPEL Ground.

The advance was down an open valley without cover of any kind to be derived from banks, sunken roads or natural slope of the ground. Consequently very heavy casualties from machine gun fire were incurred by both companies during the day.

'B' Company who had held the FACTORY during the night 20/21 November 1917 moved off at 10 a.m. astride of the CAMBRAI ROAD, and came at once under heavy rifle and machine gun fire coming from the road immediately West of the Cross Roads in E.24.c. and from the buildings at the Cross Roads. Though suffering many casualties the company gained ground up to about E.24.c.2.3. At this point 2/Lt. Castle skilfully manoeuvred his platoon and by section covering fire rushed the buildings with two sections and killed and captured the enemy holding them. The company were thereupon signalled to advance. More enemy machine gun and rifle fire opened from the vicinity of the quarry E.24.c. and road leading to it. These guns were placed out of action and the enemy killed or captured. The quarry was bombed out with smoke bombs. A further advance was now possible to the Sunken Road in E.24.b. Here however strong opposition was met both from a series of small posts in front of the road and also from the road itself. Again led by 2/Lt. Castle in section rushes and assisted by a tank, the sunken road was reached and enemy estimated to the number of 200 men were found. 2/Lt. Castle managed to detach a party of 40 who at once surrendered while all available Lewis guns were turned on the remainder who were either killed or surrendered. After re-orga again in the Sunken Road a further advance was made towards the final objective, viz the dummy line of trenches. This was reached and further progress made to the edge of the wood, compelling enemy riflemen to retreat into the wood. The Company commenced to consolidate in the dummy line of trenches but finding the line untenable and being enfiladed by machine gun and rifle fire from the wood, withdrew after permission had been obtained, to the Sunken Road in E.24.b. where they finally re-organised, consolidated and held the line. Shortly afterwards touch was gained with the 2/7th Duke of Wellington's Regt who were further to the north in the Sunken Road in E.24.a. By this time it was approaching darkness.

D Coy. & the supporting Coy. left the northern edges of GRAINCOURT at 10 a.m. and moved via the sunken Road in E.30.a. where they were held up for a considerable time by machine gun fire from enemy machine gun about E.19.c. They then moved north to the main CAMBRAI ROAD about the grid line E.24. c & d. where it was necessary to line the deep ditches on either side of the road owing to heavy machine gun fire. Subsequent progress brought them to the Sunken Road in E.24.b. and also the road in E.24.b.8.4. By the afternoon the strength of the company was reduced to about 40 men and the farm buildings around ANNEUX CHAPEL were still held by the enemy. From the sunken road sectors were organised to deal with the buildings and assisted by a tank they were cleared and about 30 prisoners taken from the cellars. The dug-outs in and adjacent to the Quarry at E.19.a.1.2 were also cleared of enemy.

By the evening the remnants of both 'B' & 'D' Coys. - they had both suffered heavy casualties throughout the day - were concentrated in the Sunken Road about E.24.b. with posts by the Quarry and in and around ANNEUX CHAPEL.

VIII. Action of Cavalry.

Towards dusk two squadrons of King Edwards Horse, who had been endeavouring to get forward throughout the day, went forward dismounted to the line of the road which joined the CHAPEL with the village. This very materially added to the strength of the line held by the 34th Coy. and effectually filled up a gap that had not been able to be filled.

IX. Action of Tanks.

These were of the greatest assistance to the infantry throughout. The limited view available to their crew was however the cause of an unfortunate incident viz the firing with both 6 pounders and machine guns into the buildings at the Cross Roads E.24.c central while held by the 34th. This caused about 10 casualties and more would have been incurred had not 2/Lt. Castle rushed out in face of their fire and stopped them, in doing which he was slightly wounded.

X.

2/Lt. Castle's conduct, gallantry and leadership throughout the day cannot be too highly spoken of. He organised every move and by sheer personality carried the companies forward with him. This is admitted by all officers and men in a most unhesitating manner.

XI. Prisoners

Company Commanders estimated that during the day some 300 prisoners were sent to the rear. It was noticeable that the enemy generally surrendered freely when the attacking force was near to them.

XII. Machine Guns

13 enemy machine guns were estimated to have been put out of action during the day.

XIII. Other forces own.

About 3 p.m. the 51st Division were seen advancing on FONTAINE led by tanks.

XIV Relief.

Soon after dusk the Battalion was withdrawn on relief by the 2/7th West Yorks. of the 185 Brigade.

The Battalion rested for the night (21/22) in rear of GRAINCOURT about K.11.a and formed a defensive line of posts. Here they remained till night of 22/23rd when they marched to billets in BERTINCOURT, resting en route in HAVRINCOURT WOOD for about 6 hour. BERTINCOURT was reached about 11 a.m. on the 23rd.

Lieut-Col.
Cmdg 2/4th Bn. Duke of Wellington's Regt.

2 Lt / Astles report of:-

The Events which led up to the capture of the FACTORY, how it was occupied and where posts were put out.

At about 4.30 p.m. 20.11.17. "B" Coy. were ordered to establish outposts in the vicinity of and making use of the SUGAR FACTORY at E.2.9.a.

The Company Commander, Lt. Knowles, detailed me to establish a post "Somewhere along the BAPAUME-CAMBRAI ROAD". It was now almost dark and I moved my platoon along the road as quickly as possible, Sgt. Kingham and myself pushed forward to select the actual positions. When suddenly I saw a body of men in column of route about 20 yards ahead. I thought this was most unaccountable and so rushing very silently forwards discovered this column to be enemy troops with bayonets fixed. Darkness prevented the head of the column from being seen. Realising that my platoon was at least 50 to 80 yards away and not moving so fast as this enemy column of unknown strength I could not attempt to capture all with absolute certainty, if at all. So I immediately decided to gain as much information as possible by some means and whispered to the Sergeant to follow me closely and do exactly as I did. Thereupon I rushed very silently and cut off the rear section; levelling my revolver at the centre man's nose and my left hand with finger outstretched as though it was a light revolver at another man's face, Sgt. Kingham covered the third very closely with his bayonet. The three tried to get their fire arms free but were prevented by my tapping all three on the nose with my revolver. They then stopped and put up their hands fortunately not making any noise. I motioned them to turn about and I hurried them back clear of the remainder of the enemy column to my own men and ordered them to rapid fire down the road in the direction of the enemy. The Lewis gun under Pte. Bradbury was the first in action. Meanwhile I questioned these captives and found that they were an Officer, a corporal and a private. The Officer spoke fluent English and I learnt from him that the body of enemy referred to above were at least 200

in/

‡ E.23.d.04

numbers and had just passed through CAMBRAI that afternoon to reinforce or relieve their old line. But not knowing the district were retiring to the vicinity of BOURLON WOOD for the night. All papers were then taken from the officer and forwarded with the escort.

I then placed my platoon as per the following sketch:-

[sketch showing positions: 5, 6, FACTORY, No 2 Rifle Sec, HQ, No 7 Platoon, BOMBERS, No 1 RIFLE SECTION, Coy. H.Q., N arrow]

Then I went to establish communication with the remainder of the Company and found them as indicated above. So whilst Lieut. Knowles was writing the report we were "in position". I not being satisfied with the positions of 5 & 6 platoons, I ordered them to replace themselves as per sketch below:-

[sketch showing positions 5 and 6 with note: "Here I established a post from H.Q. platoon to act as Standing Patrol to watch the Roads South and West."]

Then I organised patrols to keep the roads leading to South & West open.

I established communication with D Coy who were on the outskirts of GRAINCOURT but failed to get into touch with anyone to the West of the FACTORY

Then realising that enemy may still be in the factory, I suggested to Lt. Knowles that each platoon should detail one section to especially watch and listen for movement from the FACTORY buildings but not to enter them until daylight. This suggestion was duly carried out.

The enemy made frequent patrols against us but all did not escape, but as we did not capture any prisoners alive we failed to obtain further information that night.

(Sd) J.R. Castle
2/Lt.

☨ This was gamed by the Coy. Commander.

Narrative of Operations 25th November to
3rd Decr 1917.

Reference map MOEUVRES 1/20000.

1. **General**

The Division moved on 25th to relieve the 40th Division in the line. The 186th Brigade, who had been "standing by" for 24 hours, marched off from BERTINCOURT about 1 P.M. Battalion representative was sent on to meet the Brigade Staff in GRAINCOURT to receive instructions regarding positions to be taken up.

2. **Move of Battalion**

The Battalion moved off from billets at 1.45 p.m. and marched via HERMIES and road through K19 and 14 to the Canal. Teas were served before crossing the Canal and Field Kitchens sent back. Captain Fletcher who had gone on to receive instructions met the Battalion at Road junction K4D and by him the Battalion was guided, moving west of GRAINCOURT to ANNEUX CHAPEL. The Battalion halted in the open about K24D while the Battalion Commander went to the Quarry F19B to obtain instructions from the Grenadier Guards, which Battalion the 2/4th was relieving as to their dispositions. This was about 8 P.M. Owing to intermittent shelling the Battalion was well deployed in Artillery formation, but even so, did not escape a few casualties, owing to the unfortunate delay that took place.

The Battalion Commander on arriving at the Quarry Dug Out found that orders had been received that the Grenadier Guards Battalion were not to be relieved. This caused some confusion and it was not till quite 2 hours later that orders were received that the relief was to be carried out.

3. **Dispositions**

On the relief being carried out the Battalion

Continuation.

was located as follows :- Headquarters in Dugout adjacent to Quarry F.19.A.

A Company :- Cellars in ANNEUX village F.19.C.

B " in Road which was slightly sunken, F.19.A.0.3.

C and D Companies in Sunken Road E.24.B.

The Battalion together with the 2/5 was in reserve to the 2/6 and 2/7, who were holding the line in BOURLON WOOD. Owing to the increasing enemy shell fire the companies in the roads dug themselves in, in deep and narrow trenches, with high Paradors which made them practically secure from everything but a direct hit.

4. <u>Novr 26th - 1917</u>

The Battalion remained in the same positions. Intermittent and heavy shelling varied throughout the day which permitted little movement. The ration train suffered many casualties to personnel and animals that evening.

5. <u>Receipt of Orders for Next Day's Operations</u>

These were received about dusk & Company Commanders were sent for. The plan of operations was gone over and necessary detail gone into. Verbal Orders were issued for Companies to be concentrated in the Wood by 4-30 A.M. This proved to be not a moment too early owing to a delay being caused by a Guards Battalion, who were vacating positions occupied by them during the night. It was not till close on Zero hour that the Battalion was in position, F.13.B.

6. <u>Zero Hour</u>

Had been fixed for 6-20. a.m. The morning was very wet and at this hour there was total darkness up to nearly 7 a.m.

7. <u>Plan of Attack</u>

The Brigade were to attack on a two Battalion

front with the road turning north through the wood as dividing line, the 2/5th on the right and the 2/6th on the left. The 2/7 were in support of 2/6th and to subsequently leap frog through them on the line of the road in F.7A. The 2/7 West Yorks were also available to reinforce as required.

8. **Battalion Mission**

The part to be played by the Battalion was that of a Reserve Force to be held in readiness to deal with any counter attack. None however developed. The Battalion was ordered to be distributed in depth in F.13.B and coinciding with the advance of the attacking Battalion in front to advance to F.7.D.

9. **Objectives**

This was approximately on the line of the Railway in F.I.C and D.

10. **The Wood**

While the greater part of the wood was free of undergrowth, that portion to the east of the main track running N and S in F.7.D and F.13.A, was dense undergrowth, difficult to traverse and impervious to view.

11. **The Attack** ~~Enemy Barrage~~

Progress was made by the Battalions West of the Road up to and including the outskirts of the Village. Little if any progress was made on the right.

12. **Enemy Barrage**

Very shortly after the attack commenced a very heavy Barrage was put down and continued for most of the day about the centre of the Wood and the Chateau. This caused very heavy casualties to the Battalion but mostly of a light nature.

Situation Afternoon

The situation in the afternoon was generally

as follows:-

Dor W {
2/6th along road E.12.D.7.6. facing N.
4/7th in and around Factory F.7.A.9.3.
2/5th along northern edge of Wood F.7.D.
}

West Yorks
2/7th in and about F.7.D.

D or W. 2/4th in and about F.13.B and South of the Road.

No further progress was now possible and night dispositions had to be considered, which apparently entailed a falling back on the left, owing to both flanks being in the air and unsupported. By dusk a general line was gained running E and W having the cross roads E.7.D as a pivot.

About 4 p.m. the 2/4th moved up to the triangle formed by the Road F.7.D.4.2. but subsequently one Company moved to Road Junction F.13.A to form a defensive flank, touch being gained with the Brigade whose mission it had been to gain the Village of BOURLON.

Relief

About 10 P.M. the Brigade was relieved in the line by the 3rd and 5th Cavalry Regt, and moved into support in Southern portion of Wood. The Battalion was located about F.13.C where they dug in.

Novr 28th and Relief

The Battalion remained in support and though intermittently shelled all day escaped with scarcely any further casualties. The same night a Brigade of the 58th Division came up and the Battalion moved to Trenches about K.9.B, a halting place en route to billets as was then intended.

Novr 29th, 30th Decr 1st

Owing to evident aggressive action by the enemy the Battalion with the other units of the Brigade was placed at disposal of the 2nd Division, remaining in comparative comfort in Dugouts. Immediate efforts were made to refit.

Night of Dec 1st

The Battalion with the 2/6th moved to construct a line of posts extending from K.7.A.7.2 through K.8.A. to K.8.B.88. In the Battalion portion an unworked Trench was found which served the purpose & was consolidated into a series of posts.

Dec 2nd

Battalion remained in adjacent Trenches during the day and continued work at night.

Dec 3rd

Battalion moved back to BEAUMETZ during the morning, moving in small parties to escape observation.

Casualties

Nov 25th to Dec 3rd - 1917

	Officers	N.C.O's and Men
Killed	nil	18
Wounded	7	156
Missing	nil	4

A E Nash
Lieut-Col
Comdg 2/7 Bn. Duke of Wellington's Regt.

Vol 12

War diary
— of —
2/4th Bn. Duke of Wellingtons Regiment

from 1st December 1917 to 31st December 1917.

Volume 12

SECRET

12. T
2 sheets

S. Marsh.
Major
2/4 Duke of Wellingtons Regt.

Original

Army Form C. 2118.

WAR DIARY
or
INTELLIGENCE SUMMARY.
(Erase heading not required.)

1/4 Duke of Wellington Regt

Hour, Date, Place		Summary of Events and Information	Remarks and references to Appendices
In the Field	Dec 3rd	The Regt came out of the line & went into camp at Beaumetz.	J.W.S.
Beaumetz.	4th	The Battn entrained at Premicourt, & went into billets at Bailleulmont.	J.W.S.
Bailleulmont.	5th	The Bn moved by route march to Montenescourt.	J.W.S.
Montenescourt.	6th	The Bn moved by route march to Chelers.	J.W.S.
Chelers	10th	The Bn moved by route march to Vendin-les-Bethune	RB
Vendin-les-Bethune	14th	The Bn moved by route march to L'Ecleme	MB
L'Ecleme	18th	The Bn moved by route march to Vendin-les-Bethune	MB
Vendin-les-Bethune	19th	The Bn moved by route march to Chelers	MB

Stanley Major
O-Z-Comdg 1/4 Br. Duke of Wellington Regt

9/6/17

Original

Secret

Vol 13

War Diary

of

2/4 Bn Duke of Wellingtons (WR) Regt.

from 1st January 1918 to 31st January 1918

Volume 13

[signature]
Major
OC 2/4 Duke of Wellingtons Regt.

Army Form C. 2118.

WAR DIARY
or
INTELLIGENCE SUMMARY. 2/4 Duke of Wellingtons Regt.

(Erase heading not required.)

Original

Instructions regarding War Diaries and Intelligence Summaries are contained in F.S. Regs., Part II and the Staff Manual respectively. Title pages will be prepared in manuscript.

Hour, Date, Place		Summary of Events and Information	Remarks and references to Appendices
CHELERS	9/9/18	The Bn moved by rail from TINQUES to MARŒUIL.	J.S.E.
MARŒUIL	13/9/18	2/Lieut Branchard of the American Army reported for 4 days duty with instruction.	J.S.E.
	14th	The Bn. relieved the 2/4 KOYLI in the line, taking over the right GAVRELLE Sector of the Divisional Sector.	J.S.E.
	22nd	The Bn was relieved in the line by the 2/4 KOYLI & moved to MARŒUIL.	J.S.E.
	24th	Lt. Col. H.E.P. Nant went into hospital.	J.S.E.
	31st	The Brigade was reduced to 3 Batts, the 2/6 W.R. being broken up. 10 Officers & 220 O.Ranks being transferred to the 2/4 Duke of Wgtn Regt.	J.S.E.
		The following honours & awards for Officers appeared in the Ypres honours list.	
		Lt. Col. H.E.P. Nant. D.S.O.	
		Capt. R.H. Throapleton. M.C.	
		Lt. L. Cordingley	
		The following Officers were mentioned in despatches.	
		Lt. Col. H.E.P. Nant. Capt. P.L. Smith.	J.S.E.
		Capt R.H. Throapleton	
		Lt. L. Cordingley.	
		The following awards were given for gallantry (1st operations) which commenced Nov 20/17 Lt Col H.E.P. Nant Bar to D.S.O. Lt H. Gunn M.E. 2/Lt 2/4 K of Yest to Kennels M.C. Capt J.A. Castle D.S.O. 2/Lt 2/4 H Gunn. M.E. other ranks 4 D.C.M's. 4/Lt H. Metcalfe M.C. 14 M.M.	

Forms/C. 2118/16.

(73989) W4141-463. 400,000. 9/14. H.&J.Ltd.

Secret   Bn Order No. 54.

No.1.   The 186th Inf. Bde will relieve the 187th Inf. Bde in the right section on the night of 1/2 Feby.

No.2.   Advance Parties as under will proceed to the trenches on the morning of relief time to be notified later.
   1 Offr per Company & Hqrs
   1 N.C.O per platoon, 1 L.G N.C.O per Coy
   1 Signaller per Coy, 1 Offrs servant per Coy & Hqrs
   1 Sgt for Hqrs, 1 Signalling Sgt & 2 Signallers
   4 Hqrs Runners, 1 Runner per Coy.

No.3.   All Defence schemes, Trench Maps & Photographs will be taken over.
   Detail of work in hand & proposals for work will be carefully taken over.
   Lists of Ammunition & Trench Stores taken over will be submitted to Bn Hqrs in duplicate as soon after taking over as possible.

No.4.   Completion of relief will be reported in "Code".

No.5.   Coys will take over as under:-
   A Coy. Towy Post relieving B Coy 2/4 K.O.Y.L.I.
   B Coy. Water Post, Gavrelle Post relieving A Coy of the 2/4 K.O.Y.L.I.
   C Coy. Ditch Post relieving a Coy of 2/5 K.O.Y.L.I.
   D Coy. (less 2 platoons) Red Line South of Gavrelle Road, relieving C Coy 2/4 K.O.Y.L.I.

                                        PTO

2 Platoons Naval Trench south of Tony
Alley relieving D Coy 2/4 K.O.Y.L.I.
    In case of attack D Coy will man
the following posts:-
  (a) Keillor Post from the 2 platoons in
     the Red Line
  (b) Pelican Post & Halifax Post from 2
     platoons in Naval Trench.

                                      J. B. Ellison
                                      Capt. & Adjt.

Secret   Battalion Orders No. 55

(1) The Bn will move off at 8pm tomorrow for the trenches in the order A, B, D, C, H.Qrs Coys and will entrain at Marœuil and detrain at Chanticler.

(2) All movement East of Chanticler will be by Platoons at 100 yards intervals.

(3) Guides as under will meet Coys (C. Coy excepted) at the point where TOWY ALLEY crosses GAVRELLE ROAD.
   (a) 1 Guide for Towy Post
   (b) 1 —   — Gavrelle Post
   (c) 1 —   — Water Post
   (d) 1 —   — D Coy in Naval Trench
   (e) 1 —   — D Coy in Bed Line
   (f) 1 —   — C Coy at the junction of Towy and Thames alley.

(4) Rations will be del'd by light Railway to H.5.c.3.8. by tractor after which forward D Coy will be responsible for providing Man Power to push the Trucks to H.6.a.3.9. Coys will draw their rations at the following points:-
   C. Coy & 2 platoons, H.Qrs   }
   & D Coy in Bed Line   } H.5.c.3.8.
   B Coy & 2 platoons D Coy   }
     in Naval Trench   } H.6.a.3.9.

D Coy in Naval Trench will draw & deliver A Coys rations, rations to be drawn at H.6.a.3.9. Time of drawing rations will be notified later.

(5) <u>Advance Parties</u> as detailed in Bn order no 54 will parade at the Orderly Room at 7·30 am under Capt Syl... will proceed by train leaving Marceuil at 8·10 am, arriving Chanteler at 10 am where they will be met by guides of the 187? Bde.

(6) <u>Blankets</u> will be rolled & labelled by 9 am and will be sent along with packs to No 10 billet Tramway Lane.

(7) <u>Stores</u> required in the trenches will be collected by the Q'mr at 9 am; stores not required in the trenches will be sent to No 10 billet Tramway Lane.

(8) <u>Traffic Control</u>. The RSM will detail 2 men for traffic control duties. These men will proceed with the advance party & will report to the Hqrs, 187th Inf Bde H1 d.4.5. not later than 12 noon. These men will take full equipment & rations for the 1st and 2nd Feby also 2 blankets each.

(9) <u>Relay Post</u>. The Qm will arrange for a mounted orderly to be at the Western end of the Duckboard track at 11·30 am daily.

(10) <u>Field Kitchen Boilers</u> will be taken up as under, A, B, C. Coys 3 each
    D   -   4 -
    Hqrs - 2

(11) <u>Descipline</u>. Strict march discipline will be maintained and entraining & detraining will be properly carried out.

No 12:- Returns the same as last time
No 13:- Billets will be left scrupulously clear.

31/1/18

J. D. Ellison
Capt & Adjt

1. Maj Lorang
2. Capt Sykes
3. 2 in comd
4. T.O.
5. A Coy
6. B
7. C -
8. D -
9. Scout letters (2)
10. War Diary (2)

Original

War diary
of
2/4th Bn. Duke of Wellingtons (W.R.) Reg.t (T.F.)

from 1st February 1918 to 28th February 1918

Volume 14

SECRET.

Vol 14

L.a. 14.T.
3 sheets

L.I. Crosby Major
2/4 Duke of Wellingtons Reg.t

ORIGINAL

WAR DIARY
or
INTELLIGENCE SUMMARY.

(Erase heading not required.)

Army Form C. 2118.

2/4th Bn Duke of Wellingtons (WR) Regt.

February 1918

Instructions regarding War Diaries and Intelligence Summaries are contained in F.S. Regs., Part II. and the Staff Manual respectively. Title pages will be prepared in manuscript.

Hour, Date, Place		Summary of Events and Information	Remarks and references to Appendices
1.2.18.	OPPY.	Battalion relieved 2/4th Bn K.O.Y.L.I in trenches on right of GAVRELLE	See
8.2.18.	ST. AUBIN.	Battalion relieved by 1st Bn Queens Westminster Rifles and went into billets at ANZIM. ST. AUBIN.	See
10.2.18.	ROCLINCOURT.	Battalion moved to STEWARTS CAMP. ROCLINCOURT. Wiring Parties of 300 other ranks per day supplied for work under 457th & 461st Field Coys. R.E.	See
14.2.18	- do -	Band of 2/4. O.R. transferred to this unit from 12th East Yorks Regt.	See
16.2.18	- do -	Major L.J. COOMBE appointed Second-in-Command of Battalion and took over duties on this date. Transferred from 2/6th Bn: Duke of Wellingtons Regt. (disbanded)	See
19.2.18.	- do -	Battalion moved into billets at VILLERS-BRULIN for training, entraining at ECURIE.	See

L.J. Cambly Major
2/4th Bn Duke of Wellingtons Regt.

SECRET   Copy No ___8__
                    5TH. WEST RIDING REGT
        RELIEF ORDERS   BY   LT-COL. J. WALKER.
           COMMANDING   5-2-18.
                    -----

1. The Battalion will be relieved by the 2/7th D.of W.Rgt
    on the night of 5-2-18.

2. "A" Coy. 5th .W.R.R. relieved by "C" Coy & 1 Plat."A".2/7th.
    "C" "   "   "   "   "   " "D" "   2/7th D.of W.Rgt.
    "B" "   "   "   "   "   " "B" "   "   "   "
    "D" "   "   "   "   "   " "A" Less 1 Plat.2/7th D.ofW.

3. On completion of relief companies will move to.-
    "A" Coy- CHANTICLEER.   "C" Coy WAKEFIELD CAMP
    "B" "   -do-   "D" " BAILLEUL
    Hdqr. "   -do-

4. Guides will report as follows.-
    B & C.Coys - 1 per post at Batt.Hdqr. 6-45 p.m.
    "A" Coy. 2 guides at B.22.d.8.9 to take Company direct
    to Coy Hdqr. where guides will be arranged for posts.

5. Transport.
    1 Limber each B, C & D.Coys will be at Ration Dump at
    10 p.m. for Lewis Guns and Cooking Utensils.
        Arrangements for "A" Coy will be notified later.
        Cooking utensils and petrol tins will be sent to Dump
    by 7 p.m.
        Taking over Officer and party from each Company will
    be sent to new quarters to take over accomodation by 3 p.m.
        Train accomodation has been asked for, for Company
    at WAKEFIELD Camp.
        Guides will be provided for D.Coy's platoon attached to
    "A" Coy to guide it to BAILLEUL also for D.Coy. These will
    be sent to report to Companies at 8 p.m.

                                   (Signed). H.S.Jackson.
                                              Capt. & Adjt
                            5th West Riding Regiment.

SECRET.   Copy No. 6

Battalion Order No. 57:-

Instructions in case of the Battalion whilst in G.H.Q. Reserve, being ordered to move by tap, from Corps Area.
(Known as Scheme A.)

Reference Map. Lens 1/100,000.   24th Feb. 1918.

1. The embussing point for this Brigade Group will be on the main AUBIGNY – ST. POL ROAD from fork roads 500 yards W. of I in TINCQUES to cross roads just south of TINCQUETTE.
   Embussing points are being clearly marked by notice boards.
   The Bus column will be drawn up facing W.

2. The Battalion, less Transport, will march in accordance with the attached table to embussing point.

3. Transport will march, who facing WEST on main AUBIGNY – ST. POL ROAD just EAST of village of TINCQUES, behind Bn HQ 30 mins after the debussment. Personnel. Order of Transport at ready, rear will be Bn H.Q. 2/4th D. of W. Regt, 2/3 M.G. Coy, 2/4th D. of W. Regt.

4. (a) The Battalion will be drawn up on the right hand side of the road, so as to march to schedule time of departure. Men personnel will be kept off the roads at 25. – 6 yards per 50 yards of road space.
   (b) Officers will be detailed amongst the vehicles forming the convoy. They will be responsible that the embussing and debussing are carried out as rapidly as possible.
   (c) An officer will be detailed to superintend the embussing of the Brigade group.
   (d) On arrival at the debussing point, Companies will fall in and march to destination without delay.

5. The Battalion will form up on arrival at embussing point on road just NORTH of N in LE QUESNEL behind 2/3 M.G. Coy.

6. Ex. dump will be found as ordered in para. 6 of instructions for moving by train, in scheme A.
   The Transport Officer and O.C. B Coy will act as in para. 10 of scheme A for movement by rain.

   This scheme only becomes operative on receipt of telegram from Bde. H.Q.

SECRET.   Copy No. 6

Battalion Order No. 54.

Instructions in case of the Battalion, whilst in G.H.Q Reserve, being ordered to make a strategic move by road, out of 'Corps' Area.
(Known as Scheme A).

Reference Map. Sheet 11.   24.2.18.

1. Whilst in the present area, the Battalion will be prepared to move, by road, at 24 hours notice.

2. Entraining:
   (a) Entraining Station will be SAVY.
   (b) Liaison Officer Lieut. R.M. SAYERS will report at once to the Brigade Entraining Officer, with a warning order about Scheme.
       (1) Officers   (2) Other Ranks to be entrained.
   (c) Teams will probably run at one hour intervals, ie first hour starts at 0 hrs, the fourth will start at 3 hours.

3. For the purposes of the move, the Battalion will be classified as "A" Battn.

4. Regimental Transport, fully loaded with mobilization stores, will be at the Entraining Station 1/2 hours before the train is due to start. O.C. 'C' Coy. will detail a loading party of 1 Officer and 30 O.R. to be there at the same time.

5. The dismounted personnel will be at the station 30 mins before the train is due to start. The Battalion will report at entraining station in sufficient time to proceed by train as follows:—
   1st Train (No.2) 'A' Coy. 1 Cooker and team.
   2nd Train (No.3) 2/4 O.R. of W. Regt. less 'A' Coy. Cookers and teams.

6. A central Battalion Dump will be formed at the present R.M. Stores where all spare kit, blankets, etc will be dumped.
   O.C. 'D' Coy. will detail 1 Sgt. + 21 Re. to remain behind in charge of this dump.

7. O.C. 'B' Coy. will detail a train Guard of 1 Offr., 1 Sgt. + 9 men for the record train.

8. This scheme will become operative only on receipt of a telegram from Bde. H.Q. which will give zero hour.

9. Accompanying watch table gives times and starting points.
   Now detailed instructions will be issued later.

10. Upon receipt of the order to put this scheme into operation the Transport Officer will at once send 1 limber to report to each Company H.Q. and the remainder to report to the place for loading.

O.C. "B" Coy. will detail a loading party of 1 N.C.O. & 10 men to load the limbers at the Bttn. Office. They will report ready for unloading off. They will report their Company after completing the loading.

Copies to:- A.B.C.D. Coys.   Nos. 1 – 4.
           H.Q.   5.
           C.O.   6.
           2 i/c   7.
           Q.M.   8.
           Iso. Inf. Bde.   9.
           Office   10.
           War Diary.   11 & 12.

Edwl. Cole Lieut & A/Adjt.
2/4th Bn. Duke of Wellington's Regt.

SECRET.   Copy No. 6

Battalion Order No. 57.

Instructions for the move of the Reserve Division, XIII Corps, by tactical trains to ECURIE.
(Known as Scheme 'C').

Reference Map. Sheets 51c. & 36 b. 1/40,000.   28.2.18.

1. The 186th Inf. Bde. is prepared to move at short notice by tactical trains to ECURIE.
2. The scheme will come into force on receipt of a telegram from Bde. H.Q. giving times of trains and zero hour.
3. Zero hour will be the hour from which all moves of Transport will be calculated.
4. The entraining Station will be SAVY and units will proceed by trains as under:-
   Dismounted personnel will report at SAVY STATION at least 30 mins. before their train is due to start.
   Part Units transport, as shewn in Appendix Y (extract) attached, will report at least ½ hours before their train is due to start.
   First Train.
            Personnel of 186 Inf. Bde. less M.G. Coy. and T.M. Batty.
   Third Train. (Omnibus).
            Part Transport of 186 Inf. Bde. & personnel as detailed in appendix Y (extract) attached.
5. An entraining officer will be detailed by Bde. H.Q. to superintend the entraining of the Brigade Group.
6. On arrival at the entraining station, Lieut. R.H. Sayers will report without delay to the entraining officer with a marching out state shewing:-
            (a) Officers (b) Other Ranks   to be entrained.
7. The detraining Station will be ECURIE.
8. The detraining will be supervised under Divisional arrangements.
9. The dump mentioned in para. 6 of Scheme A for move by train, will be formed and the guard detailed by O.C. D Coy.
10. The Transport Officer and O.C. B Coy. will act as in para. 10 of Scheme A for move by train.

11. The Battalion will parade in the field on the Right of the road running S.E. through V.26.d. in close column of Companies (H.Q. A.B.C.D) facing S.E. (The field is close to the entrance to the Avenue leading to the Chateau).
    Lewis Guns will be carried by the L.G. sections and 20 drums per gun will be taken on the man.
    Rifle Grenade sections will be complete with Bomb buckets (empty) and cup attachments etc.
    Wire cutters and breakers will be taken.

Officers and Platoon Sergts. will carry Very pistols.

Hour of Parade = Time of departure of 1st Train minus 1 hour 50 mins.
Dress - Fighting Order.
Wireless Personnel. The following Officers will proceed with the Battalion:-

H.Q.   C.O.   ADJT. I.O. M.O.
A Coy. Capt. Kilner + 3 others.
B "   Capt. Grello + 3   "
C "   Capt. Bona   + 3   "
D "   Capt. Hucliffe + 3 "

The following will not proceed with the Battalion:-

B + D Coy. Sgt. Major.
"   "   Sgt. Morrison   B Coy.
"   "   " Eggleston   D "
"   "   " Northent   A "
C/Sgt. Buckley   A "
Sgt. Gladhill   D "

Each Company will draw out:- 1 Sgt. 1 Cpl. 1 L/Cpl. 2 scouts & snipers.
Each Platoon will draw out:- 1 Rifle Bomber. 2 Lewis Gunners.

All surplus officers and the personnel to be left out will concentrate at TINCQUES by Brigade after the departure of the last tactical train and will then come under the command of the Senior Officer.
They will include a proportion of Cooks and be provided by the Q.M.S. with a sufficient number of Camp Kettles, also rations for the following day if these are in possession of the unit. Further orders regarding the move TINCQUES to PERNES will be sent from Div. H.Q. to the Senior Officer of the party. 90 Town Major, TINCQUES.

3. Transport proceeding by road will be in charge of Brigade Transport Officer and will include Battn. Transport (less the Battn. Transport Sergt. proceeding by train as in Para. 4). The party will leave starting point (Cross Roads D.10.a.7.2) at zero plus 10 mins and march by route SAVY- HAUTE AVESNES - LOUEZ - ST. AUBIN to Cross Roads on ARRAS - SOUCHEZ road ½ mile N.N.W. of ST. NICHOLAS (Ref. Sheet 11).

SECRET: Copy No. 6

Battalion Order No. 57.

Instructions for the move of the Reserve Division XIII Corps by road to MARŒUIL - ECOIVRES - ACQ area.

(Known as Scheme 'B').

Reference Map. Sheets. 51c. & 36 b. 1/40,000.   28.2.18.

1. The 186th Inf. Bde. is prepared to move at short notice by march route to the ECOIVRES Area.
2. The move of the Battalion will be carried out in accordance with the attached march table.
3. The scheme will become operative on receipt of a telegram from Bde. H.Q. giving zero hour.
   Zero hour will be the hour from which all moves will be calculated.
4. Transport will march with the Battalion.
5. The following distances will be maintained on the march:-
   Between Battns. 500 yards. Between Coys. 100 yards.
   Between Battn. & Transport 100 yards.
6. The dump for kits, stores, blankets etc. mentioned in para. 6 of Scheme A for moving by train, will be formed and the guard detailed by O.C. D Coy.
7. The 527 Coy. A.S.C. will after collecting supplies, follow the same route as the 186th Inf. Bde.
8. The personnel of the Bde. Pioneer Coy. will rejoin their units upon arrival in the ECOIVRES area.
9. The Transport Officer and O.C. B Coy. will act as in para. 10 of scheme A for move by train.
10. The Battalion will parade in the field on the right of the road running S.E. through V.26 d. in close column of Companies H.Q. A.B.C.D facing S.E. (The field is close to the entrance to the avenue leading to the Chateau).
    The Transport will be drawn up on the road skirting the Chateau grounds, with the head at the Chateau gates. (vehicles pulled in well to the right).
    Pack Animals and L.G. limbers will accompany their respective Companies.
    Time of parade. Zero + 3 hours. Dress. Fighting order.
11. Advance Party.
    1. N.C.O. per Coy. and 1 O.R. per platoon. and 1 N.C.O & 1 O.R. for H.Q. will report, ready to march off, to the Orderly Room, as soon as possible after receipt of the order to move under scheme B.
    Lieut. B.D. Parkin will accompany this party to BRAY and take over and allot billets. They will move as soon as all above have reported.

Copies to all recipients of Scheme A.   Edw. B. Cole Lieut & A/Adjt.
                                                                                 2/4 Bn. Duke of Wellington's Regt.

March Table to accompany Scheme 'B'.

Serial No.	Unit.	From.	To.	Starting Point.	Head to pass.
1	2/4 Bn. D. of W's.	VILLERS BRULIN	BRAY	Road junction at D.10.b.5.9.	Starting Point. Zero + 4 hours.

Note:- The route to BRAY is via AUBIGNY - CAPELLE FERMONT - ACQ.

Edw. Cole. Lieut MAJR.
7/4 Bn. Duke of Wellington's R.

Copies to all recipients of Scheme A.
(movement by train).

March Table to accompany Embussing Instructions.

Serial No.	Order of Companies	Starting Point.	Hour to pass Starting Point.	Hour to reach Embussing Point.
4.	H.Q., A.B.C.D.	Road Junction just N. of Berkencourt.	0 minus 100 mins.	0 minus 45 mins.

Note.— Via Berkencourt, Incquile. Not to pass Road Junction where Railway crosses Road in Incquile before 0 minus 72 minutes.

March Table to accompany Extending Instructions.

No.	Starting Point.	Hour to pass Starting Point.	Hour to reach Chalon.	No. of train.
4.	A Level crossing 700 yds W. of Avy Chalon.	0 plus 10 minutes.	0 plus 20 mins.	No. 2.
5.	3.C.D. & J.R.	do.	0 plus 3 hours and 10 minutes.	0 plus 3 hours and 20 mins.	No. 5.

Note. Time for Transport and Loading Party is one hour earlier than for dismounted portion.

Copies to all recipients of Scheme A.

E.W. Cole, Lieut: & Adjt.
7th Bn. Duke of Wellington's Regt.

Composition of Omnibus Train.
Extract from Appendix "Y" to accompany Scheme 'C'

Unit.	Bns. Offrs.	O.R.	Horses.	F.S. Limbered	2 wheeled Carts.
L.G. Detachment, transport & R.I.S. Waggons } +1 General S.S. Waggon per Battn.	32	30	15	—
Pack Animals, 6 per Battn.	24	16	—	—
Medical Personnel +1 maltese Cart per Battn. (+1 M.G.C.)	8	3	—	3
Water Cart per Battn.	16	8	—	4
Ration, 8 per Battn.	23	31	—	—

186th Infantry Brigade
62nd Division.

WAR DIARY

2/4th BATTALION

DUKE OF WELLINGTON'S REGIMENT

MARCH 1918

Secret

War diary

of

2/4th Bn. Duke of Wellington (W.R.) Reg.t (T.F.)

From 1st March 1918 to 31st March 1918

Volume 15

L.V. Crosby, Major
2/4 Bn. Duke of Wellingtons (W.R.) Reg.t (T.F.)

Original

WAR DIARY
or
INTELLIGENCE SUMMARY.
(Erase heading not required.)

2/4 Duke of Wellingtons Rgt   Army Form C. 2118.

Hour, Date, Place	Summary of Events and Information	Remarks and references to Appendices
March 2/9/18 ECOUVRES. 4th	Ref. Sheet 51 B. Section 2. The Bn moved from VILLERS BRULIN to ECOUVRES.	J.S.L.
ECOURIE 7th	The Bn moved into support of the line in the ARLEUX sector, relieving a Bn of the East Yorkshires. The Transport Lines moved to YORK Camp, ECOURIE. 2nd Col. H.E.P. NASH. joined the Bn at the Waggon Lines from hospital.	J.S.L.
In the line 9th	The Bn relieved the 2/7th D.L.O.R't in the front line	J.S.L.
SPRINGVALE 15th Camp ECURIE.	The Bn was relieved in the front line by the 5th N.F. D.L.O. R't and H.Q and B Coy returned to SPRINGVALE Camp, A. B. & C Companies remained in support at the Railway Cutting, B.2.c. approx.	J.S.L.
ECURIE. 19th	B Coy were relieved in the Railway Cutting by a Company of the 2/7 D.L.O. R't.	J.S.L.
ECURIE. 21	The Bn moved into support of the line in the ARLEUX sector, with A B & D Coys in the Railway Entrenchment B.2.c. approx and C Coy in Huts about B.3. Central R's approx. Hd Q at B.3.b.9.2 approx.	J.S.L.
In the Line 22nd " " " 23	The Bn was relieved by the 4.1.3rd 8th Canadian R/s. The Bn moved into Camp at MOUNT ST. ELOI.	J.S.L. J.S.L.

A.L. Parke Major
2nd Duke of Wellingtons

Original
2/4 Duke of Wellington's Army Form C. 2118.

WAR DIARY
or
INTELLIGENCE SUMMARY.
(Erase heading not required.)

Hour, Date, Place	Summary of Events and Information	Remarks and references to Appendices
MOUNT ST. ELOI, 24th DUISANS. 25th	The Bn moved into "Y" Hutments, Mt Duisans. The Bn marched at 3.30 a.m. for Bucquoy, reaching there at 1.30 p.m. The Bn formed up in main with the remainder of the Division, and after drawing extra ammunition, bombs etc., moved to take up a position near 'ACHIET-LE-PETIT', the left flank of the Bn resting on the Sou 7H exit of the village, supporting the 3rd & 7th Bufffs. The Bn itself being distributed in depth with 'C' & 'D' Coys in front & 'B' & 'A' Coys in rear. At 10 pm orders were received to extend the Bn frontage and A Coy was pushed forward and to the right to form a defensive flank, this flank was further extended during the night by the 9th & 12 D.L.I.	J.A.E. J.A.E.
In the Field. 26th	At 2.30 am orders were received to withdraw at 5.30 am, 9 to pass through the 5th & 7th Bufffs Rfts, which would be in between earlier, and to take up a line L8 & 25·85 to B 8 & 0·9 afterwards Rft. Clark 5/7 DWR 1/ammo.	J.A.E.

A.Handley Major
The Duke Wellington's

Original

WAR DIARY
or
INTELLIGENCE SUMMARY.
(Erase heading not required.)

2/4 Duke of Wellington's Regt   Army Form C. 2118.

Hour, Date, Place	Summary of Events and Information	Remarks and references to Appendices
In the Field 27th	to cover the withdrawal of the 2/5th 2/7th A&SH D of W Regt should it become necessary. The 9th N.Z. D.L.I. took up a position on my right. At 11 a.m. the 9th D.L.I. 3rd 2/7th began to withdraw as a large number of the enemy were reported to be working round their right flank. The withdrawal of the two Battalions on my right flank, and the arrival of my Shropshires and three Coys 2nd S on the attention of may disposition so that they faced SOUTH. The were moved so that they faced SOUTH. The remainder of the day was spent in consolidating.	
In the Field 28th	At 4 a.m. I moved my right (A) Company to connect up with my left flank into the right flank of the 2/7 D of W Regt SOUTH EAST of Bucquoy. At 10 a.m. my whole line was heavily shelled and the enemy developed an attack on my front, but was beaten back by Lewis Gun & rifle fire. Capt J. Groves (commanding A Coy) was wounded & Lt. R.H. Sayers took command of the Coy. Wbmley Major commanding 2/4 D of Wellington	J.R.E. J.R.E.

Original

WAR DIARY
or
INTELLIGENCE SUMMARY.
(Erase heading not required.)

2/4 Duke of Wellington's R^t Army Form C. 2118.

Hour, Date, Place	Summary of Events and Information	Remarks and references to Appendices
In the Field 28th	The enemy shelled our positions continually all day, but no attack developed.	J.A.E.
29th	The enemy shelling was rather heavy, but no attack developed during the day, but at my left company engaged an enemy fighting Patrol of Officer & 20 O.R. (approx) about 8.30pm. The Officer was killed & the patrol dispersed, leaving a Lewis gun & German light machine gun in our hands. It could not be ascertained what casualties were inflicted on the enemy apart from the Officer who was killed.	J.A.E.
30th	The enemy were much quieter, generally, although there was heavy shelling at intervals. The enemy using a heavy Trench Mortar. During that evening my left Coy were given a raid by the enemy at about 8.30pm and one of the enemy was wounded. 2/Lt L. Martindale	J.A.E.

H.J.Ousby Major
2/4 Duke of Wellington's Regt

August 2/4 Bn [?] Wellington Rgt   Army Form C. 2118.

WAR DIARY
or
INTELLIGENCE SUMMARY.
(Erase heading not required.)

Hour, Date, Place	Summary of Events and Information	Remarks and references to Appendices
31st	accompanied by 2/Lt WALLER went out to reconnoitre and on coming up to the wounded enemy soldier tried to take him prisoner. The German jumped up & ran towards our trench with 2/Lt Martindale pursuing him, the men in the trench seeing an enemy running towards them opened fire killing the German. 2/Lt L. Martindale and at the same time.	J.S.E.
	Enemy shelling with Field Guns, 5.9 How[itzers] & heavy trench mortars. Enemy 5 heavy rain. The conditions here very bad. The A.P. was relieved by the 13th Royal Fusiliers 21st Sept & during the night, & returned to camp Rgt dump at SOUASTRE. Casualties during the operations from 1/o 23rd to the 31st were.	J.S.E.
	O. Rank. 10 killed 71 wounded 1 missing	
	R.J. Hamley Major	
	2/4 [?] Wellington Rgt	

"SECRET"

Copy No. 14

Battalion Order No. 59.

Ref: Sheet 51c. 1/40,000
     51d. 1/40,000

2.3.18.

1. **Relief:** The 2/4th Bn. Duke of Wellington's Regt. will relieve 11 Bn. E. Yorks Regt. in the ACHEVILLE SECTION tomorrow (3rd March 1918), proceeding by Light Railway from ECOIVRES and detraining at CABRÉ JUNCTION.

2. **Order of Relief:**
   B Coy. 2/4 D. of W. Bn. will relieve B Coy. 11 E.YORKS in CANADA TRENCH.
   A "   "   "   "   "   "   C "   "   "   "   "
   D "   "   "   "   "   "   D "   "   "   " RAILWAY EMBANKMENT.
   C "   "   "   "   "   "   A "   "   "   " CUBITT CAMP.
   Bn. H.Q. "   "   "   "   "   "   "   "   " (A.Q.A. Sector)
              "   "   "   " be at T.28.a.5.2.

3. **Route:** The Battalion less C Coy. will parade at 9.15 a.m. on the camp square in mass.
   Marching order - Greatcoats will be worn.
   The uncommended portion of the party (above will be carried on each man)
   "C" Coy. will parade at 9.15 a.m. under arrangements by O.C. C Coy. and will proceed by route march. Relief to be completed by 12 noon 3/3/18.
   All movement forward of Advancing Point will be by platoons at 50 yards interval. Guides and passwords will be carried so as not to be exposed over the top of the parapet.
   No movement over the open must take place E. of the W. entrance to MERSEY ALLEY.

4. **Blankets, Packs etc.**
   All blankets (tightly rolled in bundles of 10 and labelled), surplus packs, kits etc. will be packed at Q.M. Stores by 6.0 a.m.
   Officers kits Stores by 6.30 a.m.

1. Reliefs. Lending Clean Fty. All N.C.O's and men not proceeding to the line will parade at Q.M. Store at 8.0 a.m. under 7/Lt. Labatt.
Guard. A Guard for dumps will be detailed by 7/Lt. Labatt from these remaining. 7/Lt. Parkin to details as Remaining Officer.

Transport will proceed to take over Transport Lines of 11 East Yorks under arrangements of Transport Officer. Relief to be completed by 2 p.m. 3/5/18.

2. Billets. All billets will be left scrupulously clean. Certificates that this has been done will be handed in to the Orderly Room by Platoon 7/Lt. Labatt will obtain clearing certificate from Town Major and hand in to the Orderly Room (rear) as soon as obtained.

3. Guides. B & C Coy. H.Q. & Platoon guides will meet relief at junction of VANCOUVER and HUDSON TRENCH at 12.30 p.m.
D Coy. H.Q. & Platoon guides will meet relief at junction of MC KEY and EMBANKMENT at 12 noon.
Bn. H.Q. Guide will meet relief at junction of HUDSON and VANCOUVER ROAD at 12.30 p.m.

4. Defence Scheme. (a) Coys. will take over all Defence Scheme, aeroplane photos, maps, details regarding work on hand and proposals for work.
(b) Trench Stores will also be taken over and a list furnished to Bn. H.Q. as soon as possible after relief.

5. O.O.'s. Completion of relief will be reported to Batt. H.Q. via A.A.B. Code.

Copies to: No.1 C.O.
2. " 2/C.
3. " C. Bt. Sykes.
4. }
5. } O.C. Coys.
6. }
7. }
8. " A.O. Coy.
9. " T.O.
10. " R.M.
11. " R.S.M.
12.
13. } War Diary
14. } Office.

Lieut Col McGrey
Cy 7/72. Duke of Wellington's

SECRET

Battalion Order No. 6.

(1) A Coy. 1/7 D of W. will relieve B Coy. in FOVENT Strong Point and dug-outs B.2.b.0.2. today the 19th.

(2) OC B Coy. will send two guides to meet incoming Coy. to MERSEY C.T. where Railway crosses trench at 3.30 p.m.

(3) All trench stores, maps, documents, working parties, work in hand and contemplated ect. will be handed over on relief and receipts obtained. Lists of trench stores etc. handed over will be sent to Orderly Room (in duplicate) as soon after relief as possible.

(4) Tea ration for today will be carried on the man and served on arrival in Camp.

(5) OC B Coy. will leave a guard of 2 men over all stores that cannot be carried out of the trenches (ie) blankets officers kits etc. and the Q.O. will send 2 limbers to collect these stores tonight.

(6) Completion of relief will be wired by OC B Coy. direct to Brigade by B.B.B. code.

(7) On relief B Coy. will move to SPRINGVALE CAMP.

J B Ellison
Capt + Adjt.
1/4

Copies to
    CO
    2ic
    Office File
    File
    OC A Coy.
    " B "
    OC B Coy. 1/7th.

19/3/18.

SECRET

Battalion Order No. 67.

(1) A Coy. 1/7 D of W. will relieve B Coy. in FOVENT Strong Point and dug-outs B.2. & O.2. today the 19th.

(2) O.C. B Coy. will send two guides to meet incoming Coy. to MERSEY C.T. where Railway crosses trench at 3.30 p.m.

(3) All Trench stores, maps, documents, working parties, work in hand and contemplated etc. will be handed over on relief and receipts obtained. Lists of Trench Stores etc. handed over will be sent to Orderly Room (in duplicate) as soon after relief as possible.

(4) Tea ration for today, will be carried on the men and served on arrival in Camp.

(5) O.C. B Coy. will leave a guard of 2 men over all stores that cannot be carried out of the Trenches (ie) blankets officers kits etc. and the Q.O. will send 2 limbers to collect these stores to night.

(6) Completion of relief will be wired by OC B Coy. direct to Brigade by B.A.B. code.

(7) On relief B Coy. will move to SPRINGVALE CAMP.

Copies to
1   4/0
1   Qm
1   OMs B Coy
1   File
1   OC A Coy
1   — B —
1   OC A Coy. 1/7th

19/3/18.

J.B. Ellison
Capt & Adjt.
7/4

SECRET   Copy no. 14

Battalion Order No. 63

Ref. Map Mercatel 1/20,000.   20.3.18.

1. The 2/4th Bn Duke of Wellington's Regt. will relieve the 2/5th Bn Duke of Wellington's Regt. in Support tomorrow morning. Relief to be complete by 12 noon.
2. On completion of relief, Companies will be situated as under:-
    - A Coy. in Embankment and FOVENT S.P.
    - C Coy. in SHEFFIELD, WAKEFIELD, BARNSLEY and BEEHIVE POSTS with Hdqrs. at BEEHIVE S.P.
    - B Coy. will be the Right Coy. in CANADA TRENCH.
    - D Coy. will be the Left Coy. in CANADA TRENCH.
3. Companies and Bn. Hdqrs. will move at the following times:-
    - B Coy.   9 a.m.
    - D Coy.   9.15 a.m.
    - Hdqrs.   9.30 a.m.

    and will proceed by the following route:- Duckboard Track from ARRAS-LENS ROAD, MERSEY C.T., C.P.R. and HUDSON C.T.'s. Platoons will move at not less than 50 yards intervals.
    Lewis Guns and Stretchers will be carried so as not to show above the parapets.
4. Defence Schemes, trench maps, aeroplane photographs and all details concerning work in hand and working parties will be handed over. All trench stores will be handed over and receipts obtained, copies (in duplicate) being sent to Battn. Hdqrs. as soon after relief as possible.
5. Advance parties as under will proceed up the line tonight:-
    - B Coy.   1 N.C.O. and 1 Signaller.
    - D Coy.   do.
    - Hdqrs.   1 N.C.O., 2 Signallers and 2 Runners.

    Each company will send up 4 Field Kitchens boilers, and the Quartermaster 40 tins of water to Support Battn. Hdqrs. tonight.
6. O.C. B & D Coy. and Hdqr. Coy. will have their blankets rolled (and labelled) in bundles of ten and stacked at Coy. H.Q. by 8.30 a.m. All packs will be stacked at Coy. H.Q. by 8.30 a.m.
    All stores, mess kit etc not required up the line, will be stacked at Coy. H.Q. by 9 a.m.
7. The Transport Officer will arrange removal of above to waggon lines.
8. All huts etc will be left scrupulously clean. The Quartermaster will hand over the Camp to the incoming unit and obtain certificate of cleanliness.
9. Completion of relief will be notified by the code message "Your message 100% received."

                                                                J. B. Ellison
                                                                Capt & Adjt.
                                                                2/4 Bn. Duke of Wellington's Regt.

Copies to:-
C.O.   no. 1.
2/C   no. 2.
O.C. Coys.   nos 3-7.   R.M.   no. 11.
I.O.   no. 8.   War Diary   nos 12 & 13.
S.O.   no. 9.   File   no. 14.
T.O.   no. 10.   O.C. 2/5 D.W.R. no. 15.

Maj Coomb[?]

SECRET   Battalion Order No 64.   23/3/18.

1. Reference Battalion Order No 63 of the 22nd
inst, the Battalion will move to-day at 2 p.m.
via MERSEY TRENCH to BERMUDA SIDING –
A.D.C. central, without being relieved,
in the following Order:-
        A. B. D. C.   Hdqrs.

2. Trench Stores, reserve rations etc. will be
handed over to the 43rd Canadian Batt.
and certificates of cleanliness obtained.

3. All movement to entraining point will
be by Platoons at 50 yards interval and
on arrival at the Riding companies
will form up with intervals of 100 yards.

4. Transport. Everything possible will be
carried by companies. Two limbers will
report to "A" Coy. Hdqrs tonight as soon after
dusk as possible for the collecting of
signalling stores, officers' mess baskets
officers' trench kits, field kitchen boilers
and dixies and petrol tins.
O.C. Coys. will have all the above
dumped at "A" Coy Hdqrs by 1 p.m. and
O.C. "A" Coy will detail a guard to
take charge of the dump and to march
to MONT ST. ELOI with the limbers.

5. Handing over certificates will be forwarded as soon as
possible after arrival in new area.

                        J B Simm Capt & Adjt.

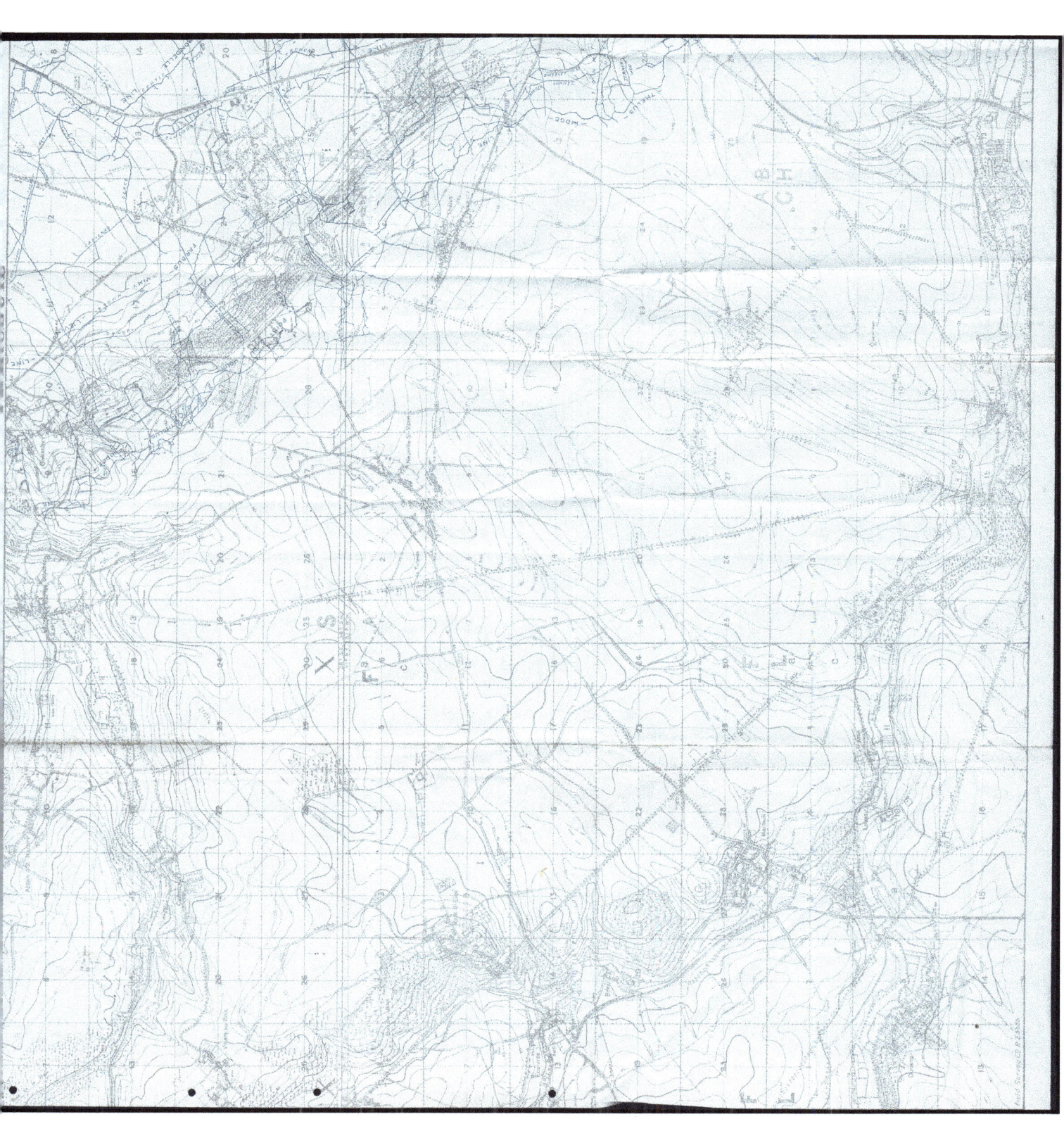

MAROEUIL

TRENCHES CORRECTED TO 30-1-18.

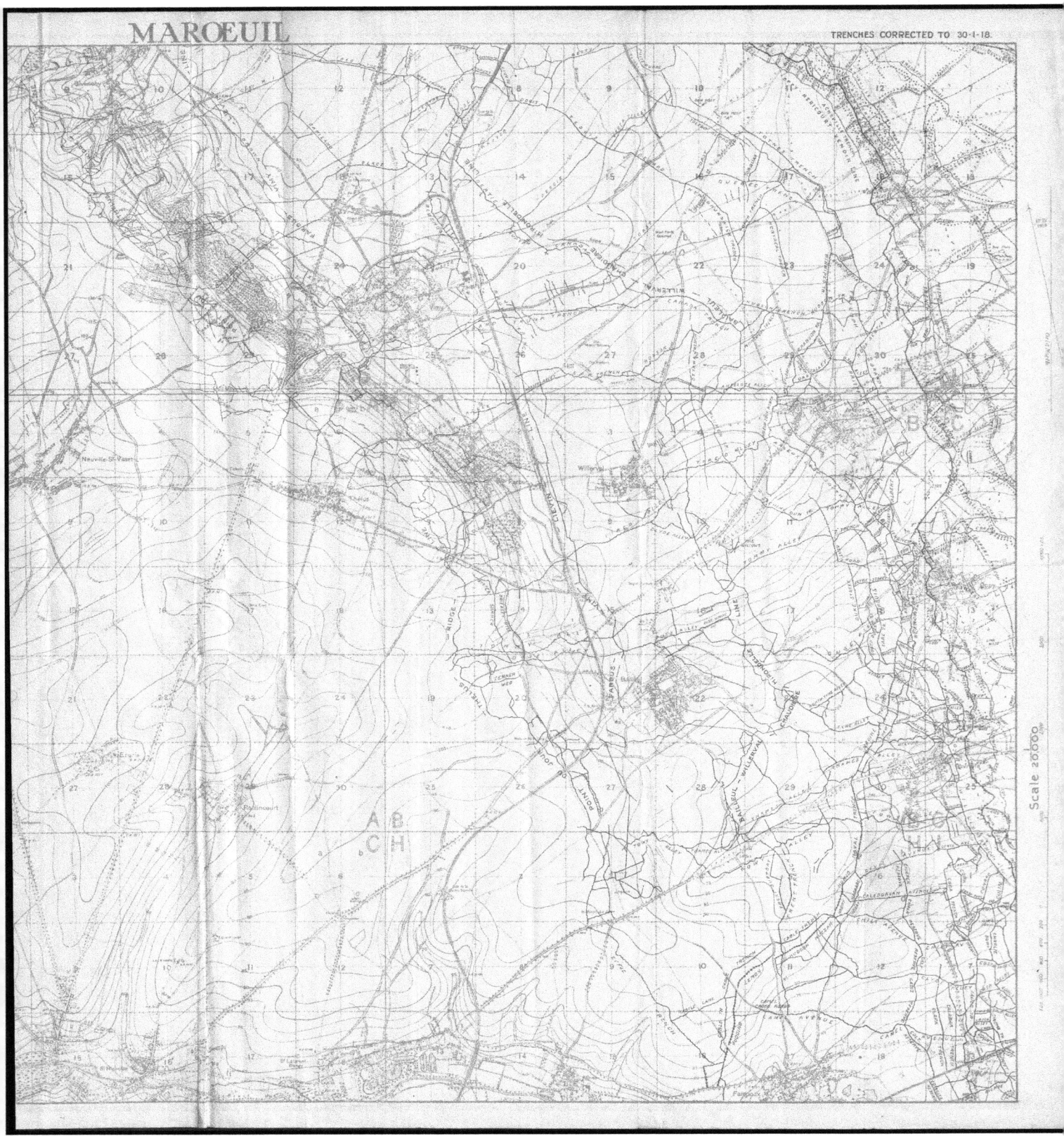

Scale 1:20,000

62nd Division.
186th Infantry Brigade

WAR DIARY

2/4th BATTALION

THE DUKE OF WELLINGTON'S REGIMENT

APRIL 1918

Original

War diary
— of —
2/4th Bn. Duke of Wellington's (W.R.) Regt.

From 1st April 1918 to 30th April 1918

Volume 16

A.S. Hurst Lieut. Col.
Cmdg. 2/4 Bn. Duke of Wellington's

ORIGINAL   Army Form C. 2118.

2/4 Duke of Wellington Rgt

WAR DIARY
or
INTELLIGENCE SUMMARY.
(Erase heading not required.)

Hour, Date, Place	Reference Sheet 57D NE.	Summary of Events and Information	Remarks and references to Appendices
SOUASTRE April 2nd/1918		The Bn. moved into Billets at HENU.	J.S.L.
5th		The Bn. moved into dugouts & cellars in SAILLY-au-BOIS in support to the 3rd NEW ZEALAND Brigade in the vicinity of HEBUTERNE.	J.S.L.
7th		The Batt. moved into support in the left section of the Divisional Sector in front of ABLAINZEVELLE.	J.S.L.
12		The Bn. relieved the 2/7 D.L.I. Bn in the front line with A Coy on the right from F28 c 8.7 - F22 c 9.3 appx C Coy in the centre from F28 d 9.3 - F22 c 8.9 appx. D Coy on the left from F22 b 8.9 - F23 a 0.7 appx. B Coy in support abouts F22 a 8.3 - F22 c 2.3 appx. Bn. Hdqrs at F22 c 1.1 appx	J.S.L.
17th		The Bn. was relieved in the line by the 2/6 L.Y. Regt and moved into Divisional Reserve in PIGEON WOOD (K.28 c 3.6.)	J.S.L. J.S.L.
24th		The Bn. moved into Corps Reserve at WARNIMONT WOOD. I 2 m.c.	

A.C.Nash
Lieut Col.
Comdg 2/4 Bn Duke of Wellingtons.

ORIGINAL Army Form C. 2118.

2/4 Duke of Wellington Regt

WAR DIARY
or
INTELLIGENCE SUMMARY.
(Erase heading not required.)

Instructions regarding War Diaries and Intelligence Summaries are contained in F.S. Regs., Part II. and the Staff Manual respectively. Title pages will be prepared in manuscript.

Hour, Date, Place	Summary of Events and Information	Remarks and references to Appendices
In the Field April 1918	The undermentioned here awarded Military Medals for gallantry during the operations near BUCQUOY between March 25th – 31st 1918. 26318 Pte Bennett F. 200920 Pte Jones A. 267405 " Firth H. 202472 " Sunderland P. 267190 " Richardson T.L. 205164 " Slavo H. 202133 " Massey J. T.306781 " Fox M. 201540 " Woodhead A. 267128 " Feather E. The undermentioned was awarded the Croix-de-Guerre for gallantry during the operations near GRAINCOURT between Nov 20th – 23rd 1917. 31749 Pte Hanser J.A. A Shard Lt Col Comd 2/4 D of W R	J.A.E.

Original

Secret

Vol 17

War diary

of

2/4th Bn. Duke of Wellingtons (WR) Regt. (T.F.)

From 1st May 1918 to 31st May 1918

Volume No. 17

17.T
3 sheets

[signature]
Major
Comdg 2/4 Bn. Duke of Wellington Regt.

ORIGINAL

Army Form C. 2118.

WAR DIARY
or
INTELLIGENCE SUMMARY. 2/4 Bn Duke of Wellington's Rgt.
(Erase heading not required.)

Instructions regarding War Diaries and Intelligence Summaries are contained in F.S. Regs., Part II and the Staff Manual respectively. Title pages will be prepared in manuscript.

Hour, Date, Place	Summary of Events and Information	Remarks and references to Appendices
BOIS DE HARNIMONT May 1st	Draft of 120 other ranks received from the 9th Bn DoWoyr	J.S.L.
5th	Lt Col H.E.P. Nash left the Battn on taking over the command of the 149th Infantry Brigade.	J.S.L.
10th	Major O.R. Nelson reported for duty from the 9th D.L.I, and took over the command of the Battn	J.S.L.
16.	The Bn went into the line in front of ABLAINZEVELLE in the left out section of the Division at Lester relieving the 4th Mx Middlesex Rgt.	J.S.L.
20th	The Battn was relieved in the front line by the 5th D. of Wo Myr and moved into support into HQ². about 7.21.c.5.6.	J.S.L.
24th	The Battn moved into the line in BUCQUOY, relieving the 27th DoWo Rgt in the right out section of the Divisional Lester	J.S.L.

Major
7 O.C. 2/4th DoWo Rgt

SECRET.

Vol 18

G.D. 1ST
Halbeck

War diary

of

2/4th Bn. Duke of Wellington (W.R.) Regt. (T.F.)

From 1st June 1918 to 30th June 1918

Volume N° 18

J.P.Wilson. Lieut Col.
Comdg. 2/4 Duke of Wellington Regt.

Original

Original

WAR DIARY
or
INTELLIGENCE SUMMARY.
(Erase heading not required.)

Army Form C. 2118.

1/4 Duke of Wellington Regt.
T.F.

Place	Date	Hour	Summary of Events and Information	Remarks and references to Appendices
	1918			
In the field	June 2		The Battn. was relieved in the line by 2/5 West Yorks Regt. and went into billets at VALLEY Camp	R.H.A.
SOUASTRE	6/18		The Battn. relieved the 2/7 Duke of Wellington Regt. in left sub-sector of the PURPLE SYSTEM	R.H.A.
In the field	10/18		The Battn. relieved 2/4 KOYLI in support of the right section of the Divisional front	R.H.A.
In the field	14/18		The Battn. relieved the 2/7 Duke of Wellington Regt. in the right sub-section of the first line of Divisional sector. B and C Coys in the front line, A Coy in support and D Coy in reserve with BHQ. at RETTEMOY FARM	R.H.A.
In the field	16/18		The Battn. was employed in depth in the night sub-section of the Divisional sector	R.H.A.
In the field	17/18		Received a draft of 5 Officers and 183 O.R. from the 2/7th Duke of Wellington Regt.	R.H.A.
In the field	24/18		The Battn was relieved by 13th Battn. Rifle Brigade and proceeded to billets at HENU	R.H.A.
			Honours and Rewards :- Appendix 'A' attached	R.H.A.

P.J. Wilson Lt Col
Cmdg the order of Wellington

186th Brigade

62nd Division.

2/4th Bn. DUKE OF WELLINGTON'S (W.R.) REGT.

J U L Y, 1 9 1 8.

Original

War diary
of
1/4th Bn. Duke of Wellington (W.R.) Regt. (T.F.)

From 1st July 1918   to   31st July 1918.

Volume No. 19

J.P. Wilson
Lieut-Col
Comdg 1/4th Duke of Wellington Regt.

Original

WAR DIARY
or
INTELLIGENCE SUMMARY.
(Erase heading not required.)

Army Form C. 2118.

2/4 Bats of Wellington Regt.

Hour, Date, Place	Summary of Events and Information	Remarks and references to Appendices
HEN.V. July 14/18.	The Bn. received orders to move South, and entrained at MONDICOURT at 9 pm.	I.S.I.
15th 16.	The Bn. detrained at MAILLY and proceeded by bus to CHALONS, and from there by route march to REZY.	I.S.I.
17th	The Bn. moved by route march to CHERVILLE.	I.S.I.
19th	The Bn. moved by route march to GERMAINE, and bivouaced in the forest de Rheims.	I.S.I.
20th	The Battn. went into action in the vicinity of MARFAUX, and the Bn. Hqrs. being near COURTAGNON. (For narrative of operations see appendix)	I.S.I.
30th	The Bn. came out of the line, and moved to the Bn. Hqrs. near COURTAGNON.	I.S.I.
31st	The Bn. moved by route march into bivouac in the forest de Rheims between ST JMOGES - and GERMAINE.	I.S.I.

D.S. Nilson Lt.Col
Cmdg. The Duke of Wellington's Regt.

Reference REIMS S.O.
   Sheet 34 1/50,000.
   Flle. de JONCHERY-SUR-VESLE 1/20,000.

At midnight JULY 19/20 1918 the battalion marched from GERMAINE to an assembly point in the FORET de LA MONTAGNE DE REIMS about 500 metres South of COURTAGNON.

At 8 a.m. July 20th the battalion moved off from this position to the attack.

The left boundary of the battalion rested on the North bank of the river ARDRE and the battalion frontage extended to about 700 yards in a North-Easterly direction.

The 2/4th Hants were on the right of the battalion and on the South side of the river ARDRE the 51st Division continued the line.

The line of the general advance was North-Westerly in the direction of POURCY-MARFAUX-CHAUMUZY-BLIGNY. T

The 185 and 187 Infantry Brigades had objectives allotted on this front and the intention was that the 186 Infantry Brigade would leap-frog through them and proceed to a further objective.

The 2/4th Duke of Wellington's Regt. moved in column of route and when clear of the Ferme de Courtagnon broke into company artillery formation. Two companies in the front line and two companies in support

The artillery barrage which was to support the advance of the 185 and 187 Brigades did not appear to have started or if so it was not perceptible.

As the battalion approached POURCY it came under severe machine gun fire from the BOIS DE COUTRON and it necessitated shaking out into an extended line.

At this time the attack by the 51st Division did not appear to have started and the left flank of the battalion was exposed.

Owing to the nature of the country the 2/4th Hants, had to follow for some distance in rear of the 2/4th Duke of Wellington's and they were not yet up on the right flank.

For a little while the Battalion seemed in rather an exposed position and its flanks were likely to be turned if the enemy made any counter-attack.

It was about this time 10 a.m. that the enemy artillery began to to open fire, but at first it was very slight and with no special direction.

The casualties were beginning to become heavy but the advance continued in two waves.

After passing through POURCY the machine gun and artillery fire became more intense but the line continued to advance.

When within about 600 yards of MARFAUX the battalion came into touch with the 185 Inf.Brigade which was held up and unable to advance. At this point the two waves merged into one and mixed with the units of the 185 Brigade tried to press forward. The companies on the left by the river ARDRE never came into touch with the 185 Inf.Brigade. The advance proceeded slowly, and being held up by several strong points and a farm Min. d'ARDRE.

The platoons on the left stormed and took the farm and another platoon took a strong point slightly North of the farm killing the occupants and securing two machine guns. On the right close to the road a platoon of another company attacked a post, took 14 prisoners and two machine guns.

By this time the right flank had rather extended beyond their boundary and were working in conjunction with the 185 Inf.Brigade. through the southern edge of the BOIS DE POURCY, meeting much machine gun fire.

Nearly 50% of the battalion by this time had become casualties but with splendid spirit they gradually worked their way forward.

On the left isolated units pressed forward to within 70 yards of MARFAUX and one platoon on the Northern edge of MARFAUX actually entering the village, but the village was held in strength and they had to retire by twos and threes.

At about 3 p.m. the advance was completely held up, and the battalion was very much disorganised, small units being well up to MARFAUX but the general line was about 300 yards on the Eastern side of MARFAUX. At nightfall the line was reorganised. On the right it was situated in the old French line and on the left some distance in front of this line and about 400 yards from MARFAUX.

On July 21st the line remained in the same position and no advance was made. Opportunity was taken to organise the remainder of the men into one unit under the only company commander left.

On July 22nd two fighting patrols of 1 officer and 20 men each went out forward to reconnoitre MARFAUX and try to enter the village. These patrols split into parties and tried to enter MARFAUX from the North and South but they met with strong resistance and suffered 50% casualties, and had to return to our line as best they could by crawling through the standing corn. During the evening a prisoner wandered into our lines, and it was gathered from him that MARFAUX was held by a battalion of infantry with many machine guns.

On July 23rd the Corps Cyclist Battalion passed through our line and advanced through MARFAUX to a position some 500 yards west of the village.

On July 24th the Battalion remained in support.

On July 25th the battalion crossed to the right of the Brigade front and relieved the 9th Bn. Durham L.I. In this position they were harassed a good deal by machine gun fire but if no movement took place in daylight it was fairly free from artillery fire.

On July 26th the battalion still held the same position.

On July 27th at 1 p.m. the battalion gradually felt its way forward and although progress was very slow, owing to the harassing fire, it advanced about a kilometre and a half and established itself in a position with its right on the edge of the BOIS DE ROUVROY running down the spur to the valley through points 173.0 and 162.7. During the night a further advance was made to a position BOIS DE NYERMONT through points 175.6 to the BLIGNY-CHAUMUZY Road at point 152.5.

Although suffering great fatigue it became necessary to advance to an objective in the old French line North of BLIGNY and at 4 a.m. July 28th the battalion had taken up a position from the BOIS DE DIX HOMMES where the track from BLIGNY cuts the edge of the wood to a a point about 200 metres East of the cross roads South of BLIGNY at point 146.4. At this position the battalion suffered very heavily from an intense bombardment and from machine gun fire from the BOIS DE DIX HOMMES and ARBRE DE VILLERS and also from the high ground North of the old French line. The men were suffering from extreme exhaustion and the advance became most difficult. However by dint of perseverance one platoon managed to reach the objective by pushing round by the BOIS DE DIX HOMMES and driving the enemy back. At this time no touch could be obtained with the French troops on the right. Another platoon by creeping forward past the Northern side of BLIGNY managed to gain their objective but were unable to establish touch with the 2/4th Hants. However a patrol went out to the flank and gained touch with the Devon Regt. about 1000 yards to the left. At dusk the remainder managed to get forward and establish themselves in the old French line. The position was consolidated and liaison was established with the French on the right and the Hants. on the left. By 9.30 p.m. the whole objectives had been obtained although the casualties had been heavy in wounded.

On July 30th at 6 p.m. the battalion came out out of the line and proceeded to the waggon lines in the FORET DE LA MONTAGNE DE REIMS.

The battalion during the operations suffered casualties but the fighting spirit of the men throughout was magnificent in every respect. There was no outstanding success to cheer the men on and the task set them was a severe one testing their courage and it is gratifying to know that they conducted themselves as British soldiers worthy of the Regiment to which they belong.

[signature]

Lieut-Colonel.

2.8.18.   Cmdg. 2/4th Bn. Duke of Wellington's Regiment.

2/4 Bn. Duke of Wellington's Regt.
Honours & Rewards.
Appendix "A"   1/7/18.

REG'L No.	RANK	NAME	AWARD	DATE	AUTHORITY
	Lieut	R.H. Sayers	M.C.	3/5/18	DRO 1302
	2/Lieut	J.H. Dunnett	M.C.	3/5/18	DRO 1302
	Major	L.J. Coombe	MENTIONED IN DESPATCHES	24/5/18	London Gazette
	Capt & Q.M.	J.H. Bond	"	"	"
	Lieut	W.C. Oldroyd	"	"	"
	Capt	F.H. Threappleton	"	"	"
	2/Lieut	J.P. Castle DSO	"	"	"
17491	Pte	F.T. Mote	M.M. Bar to	26/5/18	DRO 1359
203174	C.S.M.	P. Wilcox DCM	D.C.M.	3/5/18	DRO 1302
201254	C.S.M.	Taylor L.	D.C.M.	3/5/18	DRO 1302
31749	Pte	Hamer J.A.	Croix de Guerre	30/4/18	DRO 1295
201239	"	Patrick A.	M.M.	26/5/18	DRO 1359
24989	L/Cpl	Waller D.	M.M.	26/5/18	DRO 1359
11760	Pte	Lipman J.	M.M.	26/5/18	DRO 1359
205560	"	Robertshaw P.	M.M.	26/5/18	DRO 1359
202122	Sgt	Haigh A.	M.M.	26/5/18	DRO 1359
203075	Pte	Allison J.	M.M.	26/5/18	DRO 1359
201066	Sgt	Hipwood J.	M.M.	30/5/18	DRO 1364
201770	C.Q.M.S.	Wood A.	M.M.	30/5/18	DRO 1364
201458	Sgt	Smith W.H. DCM	M.M.	1/6/18	DRO 1370

J.P. Wilson
Lt. Col.
Comdg. 2/4 Duke of Wellington

Original

Secret.

Vol 20

War Diary

~ of ~

2/4th Bn. Duke of Wellington (W.R.) Regt. (T.F.)

from 1st August 1918 to 31st August 1918

Volume No. 20.

J. P. Mobbs
Lieut Col.
Comdg. 2/4 Duke of Wellington Regt.

Original

Army Form C. 2118.

WAR DIARY
or
INTELLIGENCE SUMMARY.
(Erase heading not required.)

2/4 Duke of Wellington's Regt.

Instructions regarding War Diaries and Intelligence Summaries are contained in F.S. Regs., Part II. and the Staff Manual respectively. Title pages will be prepared in manuscript.

Place	Date	Hour	Summary of Events and Information	Remarks and references to Appendices
ST. IMOGES, GERMAINE Rd.	1st August		The Bn bivouacked in the RHEIMS Forest.	J.S.L.
	2nd		The Battalion left the remainder of the 186th Inf Bde moved into billets at CHOUILLY, marching past General BERTHELOT. Entry St. French Army, en route.	J.S.L.
	4th		The Battalion moved by route march to OISY and entrained for DOULLENS.	J.S.L.
CHOUILLY			The Battalion moved by route march by DOULLENS.	
	5th		The Battalion detrained at DOULLENS and moved by route march into a tented camp near AUTHIE.	J.S.L.
	6th		Received 10 Officers and 257 Other ranks as reinforcements.	J.S.L.
	13th		Received 117 Other ranks as reinforcements from the 7/5 Dukes of Wellington Regt. moved into billets at SOMBRIN.	J.S.L.
	19th		The battalion moved by route march to the IV Corps.	J.S.L.
	21st		The Bn moved by route march to FAMECHON into the V Corps.	J.S.L.
	23rd		The battalion moved by route march into billets at SAULTY into VI Corps.	J.S.L.
	24th		Battalion moved by route march to the ARRAS-DOULLENS Rd and entrained to ADINFER Wood, and moved from there by route march to a point EAST of AYETTE, from where they went into action. See Appendices I & II attached.	J.S.L.

J.G. Wilson
Lt Col
Comdg 2/4 Duke of Wellington Regt

Appendix I   Original

2/4th Bn. Duke of Wellington's Regiment.

NARRATIVE OF EVENTS.

At about 10 p.m. on the 23rd August, 1918, the Battalion arrived at SAULTY by march from FAMECHON, and went into billets there for the night.

At 2.30 a.m. on the 24th orders were received for the Battalion to move, and the troops embussed at 9 a.m. on the DOULLENS-ARRAS road, near SAULTY, debussing at AYETTE at about 2 p.m. The Battalion went into bivouac on the Eastern edge of AYETTE, and remained there until about 12 midnight, when orders were received to move, and take up the following positions before dawn 25th :-

Two Companies to hold the Sunken Road A.29.d.9.6. - G.5.a.6.5. (S.E. of GOMIECOURT).

Two Companies to be in support about A.29.a & B.

Battalion Headquarters were located at A.28.c.9.8.

These positions were taken up and held in case of a German counter attack.

At about 9.30 a.m. "C" and "D" Companies, who were in the latter position were placed under the orders of the O.C. 5th Bn. Duke of Wellington's Regiment.

At about 4 p.m., under verbal instructions received from Battalion Headquarters "A" Company was sent to take part in an attack on FAVREUIL, and acted as follows :-

An attack to assist in the clearance of FAVREUIL was carried out by a Company of this Battalion at 6.30 p.m. The Company detailed was "A" Company, and the following is a brief narrative of the action. The Company marched from G.g.c.3.10. to H.8.d.0.7 by platoons at 100 yards interval, coming under heavy shell fire between G.6.c and H.7.c but passed through with very few casualties. At H.8.d.0.7. the Company deployed and went forward so quickly assisted by two Battalions of the 37th Division that the Trench Mortars which accompanied were not brought into action. The Company advanced in two waves, two platoons in each wave, moving astride the Sunken Road H.8.d.45.75 to H.15.b.9.6. At this point the 111th Brigade arrived and attacked due east from the BAPAUME - ARRAS Road, i.e. across our line of attack. The two leading platoons came under Machine Gun fire from the Sunken Road as soon as they crossed the main road and pushed on to the steep bank H.9.central - H.15.a.0.8. A Lewis Gun was sent forward by the right platoon and put the German Machine Gun out of action, about 30 of the enemy coming down the Sunken Road and surrendering. After a little further fighting the high ground in H.9.d. was reached, and two parties of the enemy surrendered, one of 50 and the other 60. The Company had become mixed up with the 13th K.R.R. and placed itself under the orders of O.C. that unit, who gave instructions for the Company to protect his left flank while he went on. This was done with two platoons. The K.R.R. penetrated the village of FAVREUIL and then worked northwards. At about 3.30 a.m. 26th two of the platoons were sent back to join rejoin the Battalion (2/4th Duke of Wellington's Regt) and the other two remained to clear the wood nort of FAVREUIL and rejoined their Battalion at about 10.30 a.m. 26th August.

Estimated casualties for the whole operation is 35 other ranks. The prisoners were about 150, but the Company had not sufficient men to spare for escort duty and so left them behind to be disposed of by units of 37th Division. No New Zealanders were seen in this attack.

During the night of the 25th/26th Battalion Headquarters moved to Headquarters at G.6.b.9.7. and the Battalion again came under its own C.O. located as follows :- "A" and "B" Companies in vicinity of Battalion Headquarters, and "C" Company in trenches on the S.E. edge of BEHAGNIES, and "D" Company on the Eastern edge of SAPIGNIES.

On the 26th, 27th and 28th there was no alteration.

On August 29th, the Battalion relieved the 2/4th Hants who were holding a line in square B.29.d. and H.6.a, orders being received to attack in the morning.

At 5 a.m. on August 30th the Battalion proceeded to attack the southern half of the village of VAULX VRAUCOURT, with a first objective on the railway on the Western side of the village, and a final objective on the high ground some 500 yards East of the village.

The attack was to be made in conjunction with the 185th Brigade on the left and one Company of the 5th Duke of Wellington's on the right.

The attack was supported by an effective creeping barrage, and although it was met with some resistance, it was soon overcome, and the first objective gained by "A" and "B" Companies.

"C" and "D" Companies then moved forward to the second objective.

"C" Company, whose frontage took in only a small part of the Southern end of the village managed to press forward and sieze their objective.

"A" Company then moved forward and consolidated in the road running N and S in I.1.d.

"D" Company had very severe fighting in the village, and the progress was difficult and slow. The 185th Brigade in the Northern half also found it difficult to make progress.

At this stage "B" Company came to the assistance of "D" Company, and the two Companies gradually fought their way to the Eastern edge. Considerable difficulty was found in locating and silencing Machine Guns which were well concealed.

On reaching the edge of the village the attack was pushed forward but considerable Machine Gun fire was met on the top of the ridge 400 yards to the East of the village, and in addition they were harrassed by fire from behind by Machine Guns which were apparently in the vicinity of the cemetery, and in the Northern half of the village.

The left Companies eventually got held up 200 yards East of the village, and consolidated on this line.

"B" Company was then withdrawn in support to "D" Company in road from I.1.b.9.5. to I.2.a.1.9., but realising that they were not in a good position to defend the line they were brought back to a trench in I.1.b. behind the village.

A counter attack was then made by the enemy who gained the Northern end of the village. This necessitated adjusting the position of the Battalion front and a defensive flank was formed by swinging the left flank back, and the new line ran I.8.a.7.5 - I.2.c.6.3 - I.1.b.8.2. - I.1.b.0.7. where it remained that night.

The following morning (Aug.31st) the 185th Brigade attacked the village from the South with the assistance of four Tanks.

When the Tanks had passed through the part of the village held by this Battalion, and the mopping up parties of the 185th Brigade were at work, "B" and "D" Companies of the 2/4th Duke of Wellington's pivoted on their right flanks, and moved through the village in an easterly direction, mopping up as they passed through, taking up their positions in which they had consolidated the previous day.

Shortly after establishing the position, the 185th Brigade withdrew from the village necessitating our again forming a defensive flank. For this purpose "B" Company moved to a position I.2.a.8.8 - I.2.a.3.7.

A party of Devons who had fallen back through the village were thrown into position forming a line of posts I.1.b.9.2 - I.1.b.5.4 I.1.b.2.9 - C.25.d.7.6.

This line connected with the nearest post of the 185th Brigade in C.25.a.9.1.

This line was held during the night.

On September 1st at 5.30 a.m. the 185th Brigade again attacked the village, and with the aid of two Whippet Tanks advanced beyond the village.

"D" Company of this Battalion pushed forward and occupied the high ground on contour 110 on the East of the village, establishing liason with the 8th West Yorks., and "B" Company took up a position immediately east of the village in support to "D" Company.

Fighting on our left continued into the afternoon, and eventually the troops on my left were driven into the village, and the liason post was evacuated. The Company Commander of "D" seeing this, withdrew his two left posts, and called on "B" Coy. to protect his left flank. This was secured by placing three posts in the Sunken Road running from I.2.a.3.7 to I.2.a.1.9. which position was held during the night.

After much difficulty the 8th West Yorks. were located and liason was again established.

On the morning of Sept 2nd the 187th Brigade attacked with the intention of securing objectives some distance in advance and North and East of the village.

The attack was launched, and as soon as the front of the Battalion was covered,"B" Company resumed their position in support to "D" Company.

The objectives of the 187th Brigade did not appear to have all been taken, and the left flank of this Battalion appeared to be vunerable.

Orders were received to advance the line so that all the high ground about 400 yards east of the village should be denied to the enemy, and at the same time extend the line on the left flank, and gain touch with a post of the 8th West Yorks. on the road about C.26.d.7.3.

By this time the 8th West Yorks had been withdrawn, and were assembling in the village for further operations, but connection was established with a post of the 5th K.O.Y.L.I. at about C.26.d.4.5. and a strong liason post was established at this point. Additional posts were put out to connect up with "D" Coy and this was arranged by "C" Coy. partially side stepping to the left and taking over some of the ground occupied by "D" Company.

This line was held until relieved by the King's Liverpool Regt. about 2 a.m. on Sept. 4th when the Battalion was withdrawn to the railway embankment S.E. of GOMIECOURT.

The total casualties during the operations were 7 Officers and 213 other ranks.

The number of prisoners secured by the Battalion was 298, which number exceeded the total casualties of the battalion.

The spirit and morale of the Battalion was good through the whole operations.

Lieut.Col.
O.C.2/4th Bn.Duke of Wellington's Regt.

Appendix II — Original

1/4 Bn Duke of Wellington's Regt.

Honours and awards for gallantry
in operations on the MARNE from
20th to 29th July 1918.

The Military Cross

Capt. W Cuthbson. Attd 186 Inf. Bde. Std. Qrs.
Lt (A/Capt.) J Stocks
2/Lt B. Stott
2/Lt A C Potter
2/Lt F K Marsden
2/Lt H A Walker
Capt. W. J. L. Hickey 2/1 WR Field Ambulance. MO attached
200455 C.S.M. Hoyle, W.H.

The Distinguished Conduct Medal

236044 Sgt. D Madden
200800 L/C. W Foulds, M.M.
10908 CSM Mann, J.H.

Bar to Military Medal

202122 Sgt. A Haigh, M.M.
201484 Pte (A/L/Cpl) H Greenwood, M.M.
202472 Pte (A/L/Cpl) W Sunderland M.M.
205364 Pte H Shaw, M.M.
167064 Pte (A/L/Cpl) J Bates, M.M.

The Military Medal

200708 Cpl. Berry, K.
241737 Pte (A/L/Cpl) E Freshwater
166167 Cpl. G. Rowley
308095 Pte Whitehouse, H.
37417 " Hardcastle, F.
33475 " Bennett, G.H.
167261 Sgt. F Holmes
167747 Pte. P. Livesey
166173 " A Broughton
167774 " B Cockerill
308063 " R Sharman
10504 " J Macshedon
267061 " C Monks
207115 " C Waterfield
306016 Pte (A/L/Cpl) G A Haigh
306966 Cpl. W Kirton
165844 Pte (A/L/Cpl) W Smith
37264 " A Lockwood.

Military Medals (continued)

202333 Pte (A/L/Cpl) S. Smith
202398 Pte (A/L/Cpl) R. Horner
26840 Pte. G.R. Booth
15775 " J.W. Lindred
266173 Sgt. A. Blackburn
266158 Pnr. Lyons, F.
203484 Pte. A/R Hart
202310 Pte. S. Blacka

2/9/18.

J.J. Wilson
Lieut Col.
Cmdg. 1/7 Duke of Wellingtons

ORIGINAL
98/21

H.T
8 sheets

Secret.

War Diary

of

1/4th Bn. Duke of Wellington's Regt. (T.F.)

Volume No. 21.

Period:- September 1st to 30th 1918.

J.J.Wilson Lt-Col.
O.C. 1/4th Bn. Duke of Wellington's Regt.

Army Form C. 2118.

Original

WAR DIARY
or
INTELLIGENCE SUMMARY. 1st Duke of Wellington's Regt.

(Erase heading not required.)

Instructions regarding War Diaries and Intelligence Summaries are contained in F.S. Regs., Part II. and the Staff Manual respectively. Title pages will be prepared in manuscript.

Hour, Date, Place	Summary of Events and Information	Remarks and references to Appendices
In the Field. Sept 2/16.	The Bn. was relieved in the line by the King's Liverpool Regt. and moved to the Railway Embankment near ACHIET-LE-GRAND.	J.S.L.
Sept 10/16.	The Bn. moved by route march to the SOUTH WEST corner of HAVRINCOURT WOOD.	J.S.L.
Sept 12/18.	The Battalion in conjunction with the remainder of the 185th Inf. Bde. took part in an attack upon HAVRINCOURT and the CHATEAU grounds. (See appendix I.)	J.S.L.
Sept 15/18.	The Bn. was relieved by the 1st & 2nd North Staffords. and moved by route march to BEUGNY.	J.S.L.
Beugny Sept 18/18	The Bn. moved to GOMIECOURT and the Railway Embankment near ACHIET-LE-GRAND.	J.S.L.
Gomiecourt. Sept 25/18	The Bn. moved to the Vaulx-Vraucourt area.	J.S.L.
Vaulx-Vraucourt Sept 26/18	The Bn. moved to a position immediately EAST of BEAUMETZ-lez-CAMBRAI.	J.S.L.
Beaumetz Sept 27/18.	The Battn. moved forward to take part in an attack on MARCOING, see appendix II.	J.S.L. J.S.L.
Sept 30/18.	[illegible] awarded during the month. See appendix III. [signature] Lt Col Comd. 1/6 D of W Regt	J.S.L.

Appendix I.

2/4th Bn. Duke of Wellington's (W.R.) Regiment.

Reference Sheets 57c N.E. & 57c S.E.

REPORT ON OPERATIONS - September 10th to Sept. 15th, 1918.

On September 10th, 1918, the Battalion moved by march route from GOMIECOURT to the S.W. corner of HAVRINCOURT Wood.

On September 11th, the ground forward in the direction of HAVRINCOURT was reconnoitred for the purpose of an attack to be carried out by the 186th and 187th Infantry Brigades on HAVRINCOURT and the HINDENBURG LINE.

On September 12th the battalion moved into assembly positions in the vicinity of SHROPSHIRE TRENCH and SHROPSHIRE RESERVE.

The 2/4th Hants. were attacking the village on the left and the 5th Bn. Duke of Wellington's Regiment, the ground on the right of this Battalion's boundaries.

The objective allotted to the 2/4th Bn. Duke of Wellington's Regt. was the wooded ground South of HAVRINCOURT VILLAGE in squares K.27.d - K.28.c. - K.33.b - K.34.a with the HINDENBURG LINE and the MOAT inclusive.

At 5.25 a.m. a very effective creeping barrage was put down and standing barrages on positions which were likely to be troublesome.

The operation was carried out by units moving from different points to their objectives at specified times, much depending for the success of the movement on one unit clearing a certain area before the next unit was timed to advance.

The 2/4th Bn. Duke of Wellington's Regiment moved off at zero plus 10, and following the 5th K.O.Y.L.I. advanced in a northerly direction with the road in squares K.33.b & c and Q.3.a & b south of HAVRINCOURT as the right boundary.

The Battalion moved in shallow columns, so that when a change of direction was made to the right, it brought the battalion into a fighting position with two Companies in the front line and two Companies in support, each advancing on a two platoon frontage.

At zero plus 60 the head of the Battalion had reached 200 yards N of SNOWDEN, the right flank being protected by posts which had taken up positions during the advance of the 5th K.O.Y.L.I.

At this point the Battalion made a right turn so as to face in an easterly direction facing the objective.

At zero plus 85 the barrage in this area changed, and pivoting on the S.W. corner of HAVRINCOURT VILLAGE advanced at the rate of 100 yards in 6 minutes in an easterly direction.

The first objective was on a line about 300 yards east of the road in the wood South of the CHATEAU. This was secured by "C" Company on the left and "D" Company on the right, mopping up as they advanced.

At this point "A" and "B" Companies passed through "C" and "D" Companies, and advanced towards the HINDENBURG LINE. There was a considerable amount of wire and undergrowth in this part of the wood, and the advance was temporarily held up by machine gun fire from the front, and also from the village.

The 2/4th Hants. appeared to have gone through the village, and were at that time mopping up.

The resistance was eventually overcome, and the final objective secured and consolidated.

During the attack 4 Trench Mortars and 2 Machine Guns were captured, and 5 Officers and 168 other ranks taken prisoner.

On September 13th the village of HAVRINCOURT was reported counter attacked, and there was a temporary falling back of the troops in the village.

This necessitated the forming of a defensive flank, and positions were taken up in GOAT TRENCH and the HINDENBURG LINE on the south side of the village.

In the early morning it was reported that KIMBER TRENCH was unoccupied, and a platoon was sent forward to reconnoitre, but unfortunately daylight broke before the platoon could get out, and by that time the trench had been occupied, and it was impossible to push forward, and after suffering several casualties, the platoon retired into the line held by the 5th Duke of Wellington's Regt.

On September 14th the 185th Brigade attacked and took a line running along KIMBER TRENCH, and in the evening the 2/4th Bn. Duke of Wellington's Regt. took over the line and consolidated.

Heavy Artillery retaliation was put down on this trench, and the wood, during the whole of the day, and some casualties occurred.

On the night of the 15th the 1st Bn. Northumberland Fusiliers relieved the battalion which marched to BROWN.

The total casualties during the operations were 5 officers wounded, 13 other ranks killed, 133 other ranks wounded, and 4 other ranks missing.

[signature]

Lieut.Col.

18.9.18.   Cmdg. 2/4th Bn. Duke of Wellington's (W.R.) Regiment

2/4th Batt. Duke of Wellington's (W.R.) Regiment. S.F.

Appendix II

Report on Operation before MARCOING Sept. 27th – Oct. 1st 1918.

On September 25th 1918, the Battalion, when resting at Ervillers, received orders to move to the area of VAULX VRAUCOURT, and arrived there about 7 p.m. that night.

On September 26th the Battalion again moved forward after dusk to a position S.E. of BEAUMETZ LEZ CAMBRAI, arriving in position about midnight.

On September 27th the Battalion moved off about 5.40 a.m. and proceeded to take up a position of assembly in PIONEER VALLEY in the vicinity of HITTEN TRENCH.

At this point the 186th Infantry Brigade halted to allow the 187th Brigade to clear the YORKSHIRE SPOIL HEAP (K.32.b.S.S.

When the 187th Infantry Brigade were clear of this point the Battalion moved forward, and took up a position in KNAT AVENUE in square K.27. a. + c.

About 6 p.m. the Battalion received orders to advance to a position west of FLESQUIERES on the HAVRINCOURT – GRAINCOURT Road in Squares K.16.d. and K.17.c.

On September 28th about 9 a.m. the Battalion moved forward to BEET TRENCH in square L.20.a + c, and later in the morning again moved forward to keep pace with the advance, to DAGO TRENCH (L.21.C.) and LAPOUR TRENCH (L.21.c.)(L.22.a.)

On September 29th the 5th Bn. Duke of Wellington's Regt. having secured the crossing of the Canal, the Battalion was ordered to move forward and attack the trench system RUMILLY TRENCH and RUMILLY SUPPORT, and then move forward to the road running from MASNIERES to CAMBRAI, with an ultimate objective of RUMILLY VILLAGE.

A few hours before the attack was to take place it was found that the 5th Bn. Duke of Wellington's Regt. had been driven back, and the barrage that had been arranged had to be supplemented with an additional barrage of 32 minutes on MARCOING SWITCH and 32 minutes on MARCOING SUPPORT, and the jumping off position changed from MARCOING SUPPORT to a position behind the Canal (L.23.a. and b.)

At 7 a.m. the Battalion was in the assembly position. The Battalion was attacking on a two Company frontage with three platoons in front and one in support.

At 7.23 a.m. the barrage came down on MARCOING SWITCH. The morning being foggy, the leading Company had taken advantage of the mist to cross the Canal over two small foot bridges, and moved forward to the embankment west of the railway sidings (L.9.b. + c.)

The rear Companies following.

The attack went forward with the barrage until it reached MARCOING SUPPORT where the barrage halted for fifteen minutes, 300 yards in front of this position. The barrage then went forward at the rate of 100 yards in 3 minutes, and the attack met with no serious opposition until it was nearing RUMILLY TRENCH, when machine gun fire became very heavy. However the attack pressed on, and the first prisoners were taken in RUMILLY TRENCH. After a little while the resistance was overcome, and the attack pressed forward to RUMILLY SUPPORT. On our right flank, very severe resistance was met with from Trench Mortars and Machine Guns, but eventually this position was reached and the Trench Mortars and Machine Guns captured. On our left flank no serious opposition was met with until RUMILLY SUPPORT had been crossed, and then the advance was held up by Machine Gun and rifle fire from FLET FARM and the vicinity of Mt. SUR L'OEUVRE.

The 2nd Division had not advanced beyond MARCOING SWITCH and the left flank of the Battalion was exposed.

Two platoons were sent forward to deal with the opposition, and captured three Machine Guns but were still unable to advance.

The right of the Battalion by this time had pushed forward to the MASNIERES-CAMBRAI Road, and a patrol entered the southern end of the village.

At 1.30 p.m. a counter attack of considerable force developed and drove the flanks back to the line of RUMILLY SUPPORT. This trench was not a continuous line, but a series of posts connected up by shallow trenches.

During the counter attack the enemy managed to establish himself between the right and left Companies and also cut off one platoon of "C" Company.

The position of the enemy in RUMILLY SUPPORT was from G.4.d.2.4. to G.4.d.0.5. Then one platoon of "C" Company held from this point to G.4.c.8.6. The enemy again held from this point to G.4.c.6.7. and down the communication trench running north through G.4.a.

The enemy had brought forward several machine guns, and an attempt to bomb him out proved unsuccessful. A second attempt was made by one of the right companies but that also failed.

After dark an Officer's patrol was sent out to gain touch with the two companies on the right and this was successful, but it was found impossible to communicate with them by daylight.

An Officer's patrol went out on the night of September 29th/30th to try and gain touch with the platoon of "C" Coy. which had become detached, and it was not until after the advance that the body of this Officer, and some of the platoon, was discovered.

On September 30th the 2/4th Hampshire Regt. made a gallant attempt to drive the enemy from the trench, but this met only with partial success.

The position remained much the same throughout the day.

A small hostile counter attack on the right flank developed about 10 a.m. but this was successfully dealt with.

At 5 a.m. on the morning of October 1st the Battalion withdrew to a position behind RUMILLY TRENCH and the 87th Brigade passed through this unit, the barrage coming down on the trench which had been vacated.

At 7 a.m. the Battalion began to withdraw, and marched to the vicinity of MARCOING.

The Battalion was composed of a large percentage of men who had never been in battle before, but their morale remained Good.

The total casualties numbered 4 Officers and 233 other ranks.
The prisoners captured numbered 6 Officers 186 other ranks.
The captured material is as under.
    34 Machine Guns.
    3 Trench Mortars
    2 Automatic Rifles

P.P. Nilson
Lieut. Col.
Comdg. 2/4th Bn. Duke of Wellington (West Rdg. R.)

3/10/18

2/7th Bn. Duke of Wellingtons (W.R.) Regiment 2/7

Appendix III

The following were awarded honours as stated during the month of September.

Capt.		N. Geldard M.C.	D.S.O.
2nd Lt.		J.A. Dunnett M.C.	Bar to M.C.
2nd Lt.		J.C. Cramm	M.C.
2nd Lt.		H. Radcliffe	M.C.
200498	Sgt.	G.W. Crossley	D.C.M.
22506	"	J.W. Atkins	D.C.M.
200874	Sgt.	C.H. Hoyle	M.M.
263035	"	F. Clayton	M.M.
306464	"	E. Redfern	M.M.
263141	Pte A/L/Cpl.	G. Mitchell	M.M.
9154	Pte	Y. Blyth	Bar to M.M.
266273	"	B. Cockerill	Bar to M.M.
22372	"	A. Bailey	M.M.
382103	"	J.A. Dodd	M.M.
235653	"	F. Ward	M.M.
201614	"	V. Barber	M.M.
205531	"	R. Heggarty	M.M.

P.G. Wilson
Lt-Col.
Commdg 2/4th Bn. Duke of Wellingtons Regt.

5th Oct. 1918.

ORIGINAL
Vol 22

Secret

War Diary

11th Bn. Duke of Wellington's (W.R.) Regt.

October 1918

Volume 22

J.W.W...
Lt. Col.
Cd. 11th Bn. Duke of Wellington's Regt.

B.M. 22.T
October

ORIGINAL

WAR DIARY
or
INTELLIGENCE SUMMARY.
(Erase heading not required.)

Army Form C. 2118.

2/4 Duke of Wellington Regt

Hour, Date, Place	Summary of Events and Information	Remarks and references to Appendices
October 1st 1918	The Battn. was withdrawn from the line west of RUMILLY the 3rd Division having moved through. The Battn. marched to HAVRINCOURT and bivouaced N.E. of the village.	B
" 2/7th "	The Battn. refitted and carried out training	B B B B B B B
" 8th "	The Battn. marched to FLESQUIERES and bivouaced in BEET TRENCH (L19 – L20)	
" 9th "	The Battn. marched to billets in RUMILLY.	
" 10th "	The Battn. marched to billets in SERANVILLERS	
" 11th "	The Battn. marched to billets in CARNIÈRES	
" 13th "	The Battn. marched to billets in BOUSSIÈRES	
" 14/16th "	The Battn. carried out training	
" 17th "	The Battn. relieved 2nd Battn. Coldstream Guards in the line facing SOLESMES. A & D Coys. taking on the front line and B & C Coys. being in support. Battn. H.Q. were in QUIEVY. (D14 c 72)	B

J.P.P.Akrod Lt Col
Comdg 2/4th Depot W.R.Rgt

ORIGINAL
WAR DIARY
or
INTELLIGENCE SUMMARY. 2/4 Sch of Instn/Arty Dept
(Erase heading not required.)

Army Form C. 2118.

Hour, Date, Place	Summary of Events and Information	Remarks and references to Appendices
October 18th 1918	The Battn took over the front of the 5th Battn D. of W. Regt facing ST PYTHON in addition to its own front. B & C Coys relieved A & D Coys. A Coy took over the line from 5th Battn Dufort Regt and D Coy moved to support in orchard N. of FONTAINE AU TERTRE FARM.	
" 20th "	The Battn took part in attack on ST PYTHON and SOLESMES (see Appendice I)	
" 21st "	The Battn relieved the 5th Battn D. of W. Rgt and held the line in support to the 18th	
" 22nd "	Left entry Brigade. The Battn was withdrawn from the line and marched to billets in BEVILLERS.	
" 23/30 "	Refitting and training.	
" 31st "	The Battn marched to billets in SOLESMES	

Honours and Awards (see Appendix II)

Appendix I

2/4th. BATTALION DUKE OF WELLINGTON'S (W.R.) REGIMENT, T.F.

REPORT ON OPERATIONS - OCTOBER 8th to 22nd, 1918.

The Battalion was resting at Havrincourt, when orders were received from the 186th Infantry Brigade to support the advance of the Guards, who were continuing the advance.

On October 8th, 1918, the 2/4th.Bn. Duke of Wellington's Regiment moved to the vicinity of BEET TRENCH (L.19 and L.20) moving forward to RUMILLY on October 9th.

After staying the night, the Battalion moved on to SERANVILLERS on October 10th.

On October 11th the Battalion moved to CARNIERES, staying in the village for two nights, again moving forward on October 13th to BOUSSIERES-EN-CAMBRESIS.

On October 17th the Division went into the line, relieving the Guards in the right sector of the Corps front.

The 2/4th.Bn. Duke of Wellington's Regiment moved to a position West of SOLESMES and held the high ground, with two Companies in the front line in squares D.11.b and d, and D.12.c.

One Company was in support in the vicinity of D.15.c.

The fourth Company was held in reserve, and was billeted in QUIEVY, in which place Battalion Headquarters were also situated.

After dusk on October 18th, the 2/4th.Bn. Duke of Wellington's Regt. relieved the 1/5th Bn. Duke of Wellington's Regiment, and held the whole front line so as to enable the 5th Battalion to organise for their attack.

Orders were received that the Division would attack on October 20th and the final objective was the high ground East of SOLESMES (W.26.b, W.27.a,c & d, E.3.b)

The objectives allotted to the 2/4thBn. Duke of Wellington's Regt. were the railway D.12.a & b, and a second objective along the river SELLE in D.6.d and E.7.a

About an hour before ZERO the two Companies detailed to take the objective formed up about 150 yards West of the railway. At ZERO hour (0200) the barrage came down and the Companies advanced.

The barrage was very effective, and the first objective was taken with practically no opposition.

When the barrage lifted, the Company taking the second objective passed through the first Company, and gained their position on the West bank of the SELLE.

This Company met with no opposition on the way to the objective, but came under considerable Machine Gun fire from the eastern bank of the river.

Both positions were consolidated, but during consolidation the enemy shelled the position very heavily, and caused some 20 casualties.

The night was very wet and dark, and although this favoured assembling for the attack, it caused considerable difficulty in locating the objectives.

On the morning of October 21st the Battalion relieved the 5th Bn. Duke of Wellington's Regiment, and held the line in support to the 185th Infantry Brigade.

On October 22nd the Battalion marched out to Billets in BEVILLERS

Total casualties during the operations -

1 Officer wounded, 4 other ranks killed, 63 other ranks wounded.
Captured Material - 1 Light Machine Gun.
No. of Prisoners - 1 Officer, 17 other ranks.

24.10.18.   Cmdg. 2/4th.Bn. Duke of Wellington's (W.R.)Regt., T.F.
Lieut.Col.

2/4th. Bn. Duke of Wellington's (W.R.) Regiment, T.F.

HONOURS AND AWARDS   -   OCTOBER, 1918.

Officers.

THE DISTINGUISHED SERVICE ORDER.

    Captain N. Geldard, M.C.

BAR TO THE MILITARY CROSS.

    2/Lieut. J.H. Dunnett, M.C.
    Capt. E.V. Blakey, M.C.
    Capt. B. Stott, M.C.

THE MILITARY CROSS.

    2/Lieut. J.E. Cram.
    2/Lieut. H. Radcliffe.
    2/Lieut. A.V. Spafford.
    2/Lieut. G.W. Barraclough.

Other Ranks.

THE DISTINGUISHED CONDUCT MEDAL.

    No. 200798 Sgt. G.W. Crossley.
    No. 22506 Pte. D. Atkins.
    201774   Cpl. N. Hanson.
    No. 34628 Cpl. H. Scottow.
    No. 34588 Pte. L. Williams.

BAR TO THE MILITARY MEDAL.

    No. 10504   Pte. J. Massherder, M.M.
    No. 205610 Cpl. (A/L.Sgt. A. Scott, M.M.
    No. 200707 Sgt. Whitbread, M.M.
    No. 22484   Pte. J. Johnson, M.M.

THE MILITARY MEDAL.

    No. 201649 Cpl. (A/L.Sgt.) A. Thompson.
    No. 263123 Pte. R. Shackleton.
    No. 263128 Pte. (A/Cpl.) E. Smith.
    No. 235728 Pte. W. Heslop.
    No. 202857 Sgt. A. Crabtree.
    No. 307574 Pte. H. Maude.
    No. 267490 Pte. A. Parker.
    No. 200707 Sgt. F. Whitbread.
    No. 35278   Pte. A.V. Allen.
    No. 22506   Pte. (A/L.Cpl) D. Atkins, D.C.M.
    No. 34578   Sgt. J.J.S. Elliott.
    No. 205610 Pte. (A/Cpl). A. Scott.
    No. 49836   Pte. H. Lister.
    No. 24718   Pte. S.C. Ash.
    No. 201702 Pte. B. Mitchell.
    No. 202236 Pte. A. Bumstead.
    No. 235572 Pte. H. Hall.
    No. 22484   Pte. J. Johnson.
    No. 34721   Pte. (A/L.Cpl) A. Cowell.
    No. 354017 Pte. W.H. Crabtree.
    No. 201630 Cpl. (A/L.Sgt.) H. Greenwood.
    No. 22382   Pte. S. Eastgate.
    No. 202046 Pte. C. Henley.
    No. 202066 Pte. C.H. Ellis.
    No. 202227 Pte. H. Woodhead.
    No. 265858 Sgt. F. Britton.

ORIGINAL
Vol 23

Secret.

War Diary
of the
2/4th Bn. Duke of Wellington's Regt.
November 1918.

Volume no 23

L. Abram
23.T
7 whole

A.S. Abram Capt
Comdg 2/4th Bn. Duke of Wellington's Regt

ORIGINAL

/4 Sidney Battalion Kgt J.J

Army Form C. 2118.

WAR DIARY
or
INTELLIGENCE SUMMARY
(Erase heading not required.)

Instructions regarding War Diaries and Intelligence Summaries are contained in F. S. Regs., Part II. and the Staff Manual respectively. Title pages will be prepared in manuscript.

Place	Date	Hour	Summary of Events and Information	Remarks and references to Appendices
	1918 Nov 1		The Battn was in training at SOLESMES	
	2		The Battn marched to ESCARMAIN prior to fresh operations	
	3 6 11		Operations (see Appendix 1)	
LA BELLE VUE.	12 to 17		The Battn was billeted in FERRIERE-LA-GRANDE and carried out training and infantry in preparation for the march forward	
	18		The Battn commenced the march to GERMANY and billeted for the night in COUSOLRE	
BOIS DE VILLERS	19		The Battn continued the march and billeted for the night in BOIS DE VILLERS	
	20 to 24		The Battn continued the march and billeted for the night at NALINNES and stayed there until continuing the march to COUGNIES on the 24th inst.	
ST GERARD	25		The Battn continued the march to ST GERARD	

J.S. Olivier
Capt
Comdg 1/4 SydH (T.F.) Bn

ORIGINAL
1/4 S/H Bt

WAR DIARY or **INTELLIGENCE SUMMARY.**
Army Form C. 2118.

Place	Date	Hour	Summary of Events and Information	Remarks and references to Appendices
	1918 Nov 26		The Batt. continued the return march to PURNODE	
	27		The Batt. continued the march to CONJOUX.	
	28		At 0001 hours the 62nd Division was transferred from VI Corps to IX Corps	
	28 to 30		The Batt. remained at CONJOUX and carried out training and recreation. Names and Awards (see Appendix VI)	

J.A. Wilson Capt
Comdg 2/4 Syl Rgt (att) MGC

Appendix I

2/4th Bn. DUKE OF WELLINGTON's REGIMENT.

Report on Operations November 4th to 1100 hours November 11th 1918.

The battalion was billetted in SOLESMES when orders were received that the 186th Infantry Brigade would attack on November 4th.

On the night of November 2nd/3rd the battalion marched to ESCARMAIN and remained in billets for the night.

At midnight November 3rd/4th the Brigade moved forward and took over the right half of the Divisional front, from the 187th Infantry Brigade.

The battalion left ESCARMAIN at midnight November 3rd/4th and moved forward along a track which had been taped out and assembled in the Sunken Road in R20 d & R26 b. The ground had been reconnoitred the day before and there was no difficulty in reaching the position.

The 2/4th Hampshire Regiment were to take the 1st objective from R18 c.3.0. to R11 d.7.0. The 2/4th Duke of Wellington's Reg't the 2nd objective on the line of road M15 d.1.0. - M15 b.5.0. - M9 d.8.0. with an intermediate objective at M14 d.6.0. - M8 d.8.0. The 5th Duke of Wellington's Reg't the 3rd and final objective about M18 c.7.0. to M12 c.1.0.

The barrage that came down at Zero hour (0530 hours) was exceedingly heavy and effective. At zero hour the 2/4th Duke of Wellington's moved forward in column of route with platoons at intervals, to positions in rear of the 2/4th Hampshire Reg't. The enemy retaliated with considerable shell fire and several casualties were caused in two platoons of the leading company.

At about the railway it became necessary to go forward in Artillery formation as this point was apparently the barrage line of the enemy.

The jumping off position in rear of the Hampshire Reg't was reached well before time and the leading companies passed through as soon as the Hampshires gained their objective.

The battalion attacked on a two company frontage with three platoons in front and one in support. At 0751 hours the leading companies passed through the Hampshire Reg't. The right company met with harassing fire from machine guns from the start but gradually worked forward capturing several MG and killing the gun crews.

North of RAMPONEAU the enemy tried to hold their ground but resistance was soon overcome and 30 prisoners taken.

The objective was reached well up behind the barrage and the position consolidated.

The left company met with bitter opposition at first but on reaching the river RHONELLE the eastern bank was strongly held. The enemy were immediately engaged with Lewis gun fire whilst platoons crossed the river which was in places 30 inches deep.

Two platoons worked round and outflanked the position whilst the third platoon mopped up.

The company then advanced to La BELLE MAISON FARM and heavy machine gun fire and trench mortars were met. Two field guns were also close to this position firing at point blank range. The centre platoon worked forward under cover of the walls and entered the house capturing 4 machine guns and killing a number of the enemy.

Under cover of the barrage the company advanced and captured a number of the enemy in the sunken road M14 a. & b.; the left platoon up the sunken road in M8 d. & captured two field guns and reached their objective.

The rear companies then passed through the leading companies and proceeded towards the final objective of the battalion. The right support proceeded some distance meeting only slight opposition from machine gun fire but on reaching a position about M15 c.6.6. were held up but eventually overcame the resistance and captured three officers & 73 other ranks together with 10 machine guns. About 1015 hours the intermediate objective on the right was procured.

The left support company advanced without much opposition until it reached its objective, when considerable machine gun fire was met. This was eventually overcome and the consolidation was completed. The final objective having been reached the 5th Duke of Wellington's Reg't passed through.

On November 5th the battalion re-organized and marched to Hitensart.

On November 6th the battalion again moved forward and proceeded to take up a position in the Road N10 c. & N15.b.

The roads were bad through the rain and the main Artillery had not moved forward.

One Brigade of Artillery was attached to the 186th Infantry Brigade & one section attached to each battalion in the front line. On reaching the assembly position information was received that the 185th Infantry Brigade had reached a line west of RAV du LOUVON and orders were received for the 2/4th Hampshire Reg't & 2/4th Duke of Wellington's Reg't to move forward and attack.

The attack was planned with the 2/4th Duke of Wellington's on the right and 2/4th Hampshires on the left. Four objectives were given, companies to leapfrog twice to the final objective.

The attack started at 1130 hours and this battalion attacked on a two company frontage with three platoons in the front and one in support. Very little opposition was met and the first objective east of the RAV de MECQUIGNIES O14 b. & d. was reached at 1230 hours. The rear companies then passed through but the advance was slow owing to the difficulty of the enclosed country and the weather conditions.

A certain amount of Artillery fire was met and a slight amount of machine gun fire.

The second objective the road in O15 b.& d. was reached before dusk and it was decided not to continue the advance that night. On November 7th the 5th Duke of Wellington's and 8th West Yorks and the 5th Devons continued the advance.

The battalion was then withdrawn into billets at La GRAND RUE-BOTTIAU & La CHAUSSEE.

On November 9th the battalion moved to SOUS le BOIS and on the morning of the 10th took over the outpost line from the 2/4th York and Lancaster Reg't in front of LOUVROUIL in Q15 & 16. This line forming a defensive flank. On November 11th the line was advanced and an outpost position taken up to the East of the river Solre in Q17 d. & Q18 a.. The total advance made by the Division since November 4th is 17 miles.

At 1100 hours hostilities ceased an armistice having been signed.

Captures:-

Prisoners, 5 Officers 259 other ranks.

Material, 2-77mm Field Guns, 32 Machine Guns, Trench Mortars 5, 1 Anti-Tank Rifle.

Casualties.   Officers.   Other ranks.

killed.   2   17
wounded. (x)   3   94
(x) 1 since died of wounds.
missing.   Nil.   21

11th November 1918

Lieut-Colonel,
Commanding 2/4th Bn DUKE OF WELLINGTON'S REGIMENT.

Appendix II

HONOURS AND AWARDS – NOVEMBER, 1918.

Officers.

Rank.	Name.	Award.	Authority.
Captain	B.C. LUPTON, M.C.	Bar to M.C.	D.R.O. 1645 d/d 19.11.1
Second Lieutenant (Acting Captain)	H.J. BILSBOROUGH.	M.C.	D.R.O. 1645 d/d 19.11.18

Other Ranks.

		Award	Authority
No. 22484 Pte.	Johnson, J., M.M.	Bar to M.M.	D.R.O. 1616 d/d 1.11.18.
" 34327 "	Cleghorn, R.	D.C.M.	D.R.O. 1645 d/d 19.11.18.
" 201649 Sgt.	Thompson, A.	D.C.M.	D.R.O. 1645 d/d 19.11.18.

2.12.18.

Capt.
Cmdg. 2/4th. Bn. Duke of Wellington's Regt.

Secret.

War Diary
of
2/4th Battn. Duke of Wellington's Regt.

Volume No. 24 — December 1918.

G.J. Wilson
Lieut-Col.
Comdg. 2/4 Bn. Duke of Wellington's Regt.

WAR DIARY
or
INTELLIGENCE SUMMARY.
(Erase heading not required.)

Army Form C. 2118.

ORIGINAL

2/4 Duke of Wellington's Regt.

Place	Date	Hour	Summary of Events and Information	Remarks and references to Appendices
	1918		MARCH into GERMANY continued.	
Conjoux	Dec 1		The Batt" was in war at Conjoux	J.A.C.
"	6th		The Batt" moved to LEIGNON.	J.A.C.
LEIGNON	9/10		The Batt" moved to FAILON	J.A.C.
FAILON	11th		The Batt" moved to OCQUIER	J.A.C.
OCQUIER	12th		The Batt" moved to the village of PEROT MALACORD and HOUPET	J.A.C.
HOUPET	13th		The Batt" moved to RAHIER	J.A.C.
RAHIER	14th		The Batt" moved to PETIT HALLEUX, and rested there for one day	J.A.C.
PETIT HALLEUX	16th		The Batt" moved to VILLE DU BOIS	J.A.C.
VILLE DU BOIS	17th		The Batt" crossed the Belgium frontier into GERMANY, and rested at DEIDENBURG.	J.A.C.
Deidenburg	22nd		The Batt" moved to BULLINGEN	J.A.C.
BULLINGEN	23rd		The Batt" moved to HOLLERATH.	J.A.C.
HOLLERATH	24th		The Batt" moved to SOTENICH	J.A.C.
SOTENICH	25th		The Batt" moved to the Major Reggendorf a STREMPT the Battalions final destination. E.C.S.D. Coy & H.Q.s and Lewis Guns went into the former village and A, B Coys & Transport into the latter village	J.A.C.

WAR DIARY
or
INTELLIGENCE SUMMARY.

(Erase heading not required.)

Army Form C. 2118.

ORIGINAL

1/4 Duke of Wellington's Regt

Place	Date	Hour	Summary of Events and Information	Remarks and references to Appendices
Roggendorf	Dec 23rd	Colonel	The weather during the month of December was very bad and it rained nearly every day. That the Battn was moving. The scale for the first part of the journey were good, but during the latter part of the march they were very bad. The transport came through the journey exceptionally well. There were no breakdowns or failures in any way. The spirits of the troops during the march was excellent in spite of the long marches in bad weather in bad roads. The first batch of men were appointed for demobilisation. List of names for the month of December are attached as Appendix L.	M.G. M.G. M.G.
Roggendorf	28			

J.J. Wilson Lt Col
Comdg 1/4 Duke of Wellington's Regt

APPENDIX I.

2/4th Battn. Duke of Wellington's Regiment.

List of Honours and Awards - December 1918.

		Awarded.
202133 Pte. Massey J.T. M.M.		La Medaille Militaire.
34578 C.S.M. Elliott J.J.S.	M.M.	Bar to M.M.
34507 Pte. Crabtree W.H.	M.M.	Bar to M.M.
306764 Sgt. Readfearn E.	M.M.	Bar to M.M.
201544 L/C. Matthews P.		M.M.
34720 Pte. Carden J.		M.M.
265479 C.S.M. Peacock E.		M.M.
22367 Pte. Tranter W.		M.M.
24135 " Rodgers J.		M.M.
34860 " McGarvey M.		M.M.
40086 " Reay J.L.T.		M.M.
201000 Sgt. Hey H.		M.M.
200735 Sgt. Greenwood E.		M.M.

P.J. Wilson

Lieut-Col.
Cmdg. 2/4th Bn. Duke of Wellington's Regt.

Secret

Original

7th Duke of Wellington's (W.R.) Regiment (T.F.)

War Diary

1st to 31st January 1919

Volume XXV

Sent.

Original

WAR DIARY
or
INTELLIGENCE SUMMARY.
(Erase heading not required.)

Army Form C. 2118.

Instructions regarding War Diaries and Intelligence Summaries are contained in F. S. Regs., Part II. and the Staff Manual respectively. Title pages will be prepared in manuscript.

Place	Date	Hour	Summary of Events and Information	Remarks and references to Appendices
ROGGENDORF GERMANY	1/1/19 31/1/19		The Battalion was situated in billets during the month of January, two Companies & Headquarters in the village of ROGGENDORF and two Companies in the village of STREMPT.	OC

2/2/19

J.E.F. Nixon Lot-Col
OC 1/4 Duke of Wellingtons Regt.

2/4 Bn Duke of Wellington's (WR) Regt (TF)

APPENDIX No 1 — Honours & Awards
January 1919

REGL No	RANK	NAME	AWARD	DATE	AUTHORITY
	Lieut-Colonel	P.P. Wilson, DSO	Croix de Guerre Silver Star	16-1-19	D.R.O. 1783
	Capt	J.B. Ellison	— do —	"	— do —
	2/Lt	R. Duckett	Military Cross	24-1-19	D.R.O. 1808
	"	M. Hully	— do —	"	— do —
	Capt	J.B. Ellison	M.I.D	28/1/19	D.R.O. 1820
24069	Pte	Price R.	Croix de Guerre Silver Star	16-1-19	" 1783
201416	"	Isherwood J.W	do Bronze Star	"	" "
201273	Sgt	Harrison E	M.S.M.	28/1/19	" 1820
201295	Sgt	Nettleton F.	do	"	" "
202940	R.Q.M.S	Lowes W.R.	do	"	" "
200860	C.Q.M.S.	Brooke P.	M.I.D.	"	" "

2/2/1919

P.P. Wilson
Lieut Col
Cmg 2/4 Duke of Wellington's Regt

No. 26
Original

Secret

WD 26

War Diary
of the
2/4 Bn Duke of Wellington's (W.R.) Regiment (T.F.)

from

1st February 1919

to

28th February 1919

R.P. Wilson
Lieut-Colonel
2/4 Duke of Wellington's (W.R.) Regt (T.F.)

28/2/1919

Army Form C. 2118.

WAR DIARY
or
INTELLIGENCE SUMMARY.
(Erase heading not required.)

Instructions regarding War Diaries and Intelligence Summaries are contained in F. S. Regs., Part II. and the Staff Manual respectively. Title pages will be prepared in manuscript.

Place	Date	Hour	Summary of Events and Information	Remarks and references to Appendices
Roggendorf Germany	1/2/19 to 21/2/19		The Battalion remained in billets in ROGGENDORF until the morning of 22nd February 1919	R. Compy. Cs.
Zulpich Germany	22/2/19 to 28/2/19		The Battalion on instructions received from 62nd Division, through 186 Infantry Brigade, proceeded by route march on the morning of the 22nd February to the ZULPICH area to join the 16th Infantry Brigade, 6th Division, with Battalion Headquarters in ZULPICH.	R. Compy. Cs.

28/2/1919

E. J. Nixon
Lieut-Colonel
4 Du Duke of Wellington (WR) Regt (T.F.)

T2131. Wt. W708-776. 500000. 4/15. Sir J. C. & S.

Appendix 1.

2/4TH BN. DUKE OF WELLINGTON'S (W.R.) REGT.

HONOURS AND AWARDS - FEBRUARY.

N I L.

[signature]
Lieut. Col.,
Cmdg. 2/4th Bn. Duke of Wellington's Regt.

28.2.19.

www.ingramcontent.com/pod-product-compliance
Lightning Source LLC
Chambersburg PA
CBHW081410160426
43193CB00013B/2145